A HISTORY OF

THEATER
— *on* —
CAPE COD

A HISTORY OF
THEATER
— *on* —
CAPE COD

SUE MELLEN

Foreword by Kathi Scrizzi Driscoll

THE
History
PRESS

Published by The History Press
Charleston, SC
www.historypress.com

Front cover: Michael and Suz Karchmer; *inset, top left*: courtesy CLOC staff; *inset, top right*: William L. Smith Photography.
Back cover: Needpix.com.

First published 2020

Manufactured in the United States

ISBN 9781467142878

Library of Congress Control Number: 2020931968

Notice: The information in this book is true and complete to the best of our knowledge. It is offered without guarantee on the part of the author or The History Press. The author and The History Press disclaim all liability in connection with the use of this book.

This book is dedicated, as in all things in my life, to my children, Lynne, Leigh, Nedal and Suna, who have always given me the sense of purpose I need to reach for the heights.

Thanks to family and friends who gave me the love and support I needed to make it to the last page.

And a special nod to everyone who has ever stepped foot on a stage; without them the world would be a much less colorful place.

CONTENTS

Foreword

MORE THAN 100 YEARS OF HISTORY MAKES LIVE THEATER KEY PART OF CAPE COD'S UNIQUE IDENTITY

It is sixty-three miles from the Sagamore Bridge in Bourne to the Pilgrim Monument in Provincetown, and within the fifteen Cape Cod towns that surround that route are about two dozen live theaters and an ever-changing number of theater groups that perform in shared or borrowed spaces. Add in visiting and pop-up performances that fill summer and off-season schedules, and some towns have two, three or even four places to regularly watch theater.

Pretty much any night of the busy Cape Cod summer season from Memorial Day to Labor Day, a theater fan could have several—if not a dozen—choices of musicals, comedies or dramas to watch on area stages. More than one hundred shows are presented in June, July and August alone.

That unusual wealth doesn't count the busy middle- and high-school performing arts programs training the next generations. Take a short ferry ride to nearby islands Martha's Vineyard and Nantucket, and you'll find more performing theater groups, too.

This vibrant live performance scene grows out of a long and varied history, developing over the years into a vital part of the Cape's "creative economy" and unique identity. "The arts are the Cape," Anita Walker, executive director of the state's Mass Cultural Council, told a group of arts leaders gathered in Provincetown in 2017. "This is who you are. This is why you live here. This is why people come here. The arts are the bedrock of your economy."

Theaters are among about four hundred Cape nonprofit arts-related organizations, according to 2018 data from the Arts Foundation of Cape Cod. Cultural tourism is the fastest-growing sector of the travel industry, statistics for Barnstable County show.

The state's cultural council has supported numerous Cape theaters, and their building projects, and has repeatedly recognized the area's overall commitment to the arts. Of the forty-nine Cultural Districts designated throughout Massachusetts since 2011, nine of them—almost 20 percent— are on the small Cape Cod arm of land that extends into the ocean off the state's eastern coast and the two islands beyond to the south.

Such cultural districts "help local arts, humanities, and science organizations improve the quality and range of their public programs so that more local families can benefit from them," the council notes. "They enhance the experience for visitors and thus attract more tourist dollars and tax revenue. And they attract artists, cultural organizations, and entrepreneurs of all kinds—enhancing property values and making communities more attractive."

For theater, more than 600,000 people attend performances in the region every year, according to 2018 figures from the Cape and Islands Theater Coalition, with thousands more serving as volunteers and donors. What's offered includes community theater, where your dentist or favorite baker may be on stage; family theaters with children learning the craft and life lessons; training programs for college students from across the country (nine shows in nine summer weeks!); and shows with professional, working actors and even Broadway and TV stars.

Some theater companies have long records here. The professional Cape Playhouse in Dennis is entering its ninety-fourth season; Barnstable Comedy Club community theater (which once counted author Kurt Vonnegut among its members) is producing its ninety-eighth season; College Light Opera Company in Falmouth just celebrated fifty-two years of training students; and Harwich Junior Theatre, now doing business as the Cape Cod Theatre Company, is in its sixty-ninth season of producing shows with and for young people and adults in West Harwich.

In Barnstable County in 2018, there were 7,392 people employed in creative jobs, either full- or part-time year-round—a number 22 percent above the national county average, according to data from the foundation and the Mass Hire/Cape & Islands Workforce Board.

And state statistics show that cultural tourists have higher levels of income and spend $62 more per day and $200 more per trip than other travelers. Cultural tourists also include multiple destinations during a visit and stay longer at each destination. Patrons of the arts spend their money around their artistic experiences on dining, lodging, childcare and transportation.

Despite the positive economic impact of cultural tourism, even longstanding theater companies are finding it challenging to survive in an age when all kinds of electronic media compete for audiences' attention. This can be an especially vexing problem in an area with such a richness of choices. So, at some companies, officials are working to develop new kinds of organizations—sometimes reinventing themselves as arts centers and at other times exploring the possibility of partnerships—to improve their odds for survival.

Why work so hard to save theaters? Beyond the cultural and economic importance, a big reason is that so many believe in the importance of a shared experience. On Cape Cod, that can be a classic comedy or a new drama, a night of Shakespeare or an afternoon of Rodgers and Hammerstein. It can be as light as a frothy musical romance on a star-filled balmy July night as part of a memorable vacation. Or it can be as important as group consideration of topics like racism or domestic abuse through hearing and watching a story being told.

"There are great works of art that bring us all together [to] reassess who and what we are," David Drake, artistic director at The Provincetown Theater, said in fall 2018 when his company presented a play about the hate-crime murder of a gay teen. A play can be "a great way to listen to opinions and ideas that you don't necessarily agree with."

"The saying is that 'live theater transforms lives' because you're feeling something together," said Nina Schuessler, artistic director of the Cape Cod Theatre Company/Home of the Harwich Junior Theatre, who was producing a show about addiction and recovery. "When you're in an audience, it's a shared experience. That's what makes it so powerful."

And when you work in theater, it's a shared experience too. Open any backstage door at a Cape Cod theater and you'll hear story after story from cast and crew members about the personal value of being part of a show.

Patrons are entertained and often enriched by the stories they hear, but the creative people who offer those shows are sometimes even more enriched by helping to tell them. Working to "put on a show" means becoming part of a team—and, to some, a family. People often forge strong friendships when they are part of a community working toward a common goal of giving something to the people in the audience.

That can be a powerful—to some, a life-changing—lesson and opportunity for young and old. For some, theater is a job that is meaningful to them for many reasons; to the many other volunteers involved simply for the love of it, theater can make their life better.

When the Cape Cod Theatre Company recently suffered financial woes, it was the alumni of now-grown children who performed and took classes there over the decades who were key to rallying support to save it.

"That place made such an impact on my life. I know I wouldn't be here doing what I'm doing [without it]," Will Hopper, a designer whose work includes the TV series *The Americans*, said at the time. "It's a safe haven and it should be there for people who haven't discovered it yet."

—Kathi Scrizzi Driscoll,
entertainment editor/arts writer, *Cape Cod Times*

ACKNOWLEDGEMENTS

It seems an almost impossible task to acknowledge everyone who shared with me their knowledge and wisdom as I put the myriad pieces of this book together.

Here's my attempt:

Thanks to Diana Batchelor and other staff at the Pilgrim Monument and Provincetown Museum for taking the time to tell me the story of theater in Provincetown and share pictures of the wonderful pieces in their exhibit.

Thanks to Meg Costello, research manager at Falmouth Museum on the Green, for literally opening her archives for me.

It would have been impossible to write this book without the work of the following writers always within reach:

The legendary *Cape Cod Times* theater and nightlife writer Evelyn Lawson, whose book *Theater on Cape Cod* was my Bible through this project. I suspect she is spending eternity sitting in a beautifully appointed theater with notebook and pen in hand.

Mary Heaton Vorse, whose book *Time and the Town* is virtually the Provincetown Bible.

Dr. Jeffrey Kennedy, whose online work *A History of the Provincetown Playhouse* chronicles the history of the original Provincetown Players.

David Kaplan, curator of the Tennessee Williams Festival, whose book *Tennessee Williams in Provincetown* spins the tale of the master's relationship with the town at the tip of the Cape. Kaplan was a font of both information and enthusiasm.

Marcia Monbleau, whose book *The Cape Playhouse* was indispensable in writing about such an important part of Cape theater history.

Robert Davis, whose *A History of Monomoy Theatre* tells the wonderful story of Chatham's theater.

Paul Driscoll, whose book *25 Years at Highfield: A History of the College Light Opera Company* is a comprehensive look at theater history in fabulous Falmouth.

DeWitt C. Jones III, whose article in the 1990 *Spiritsail* magazine, "Theatre in Falmouth over the Past 70 Years," was a treasure trove of information.

Carolyn Lloyd, whose "Celebrating 50 Years of the College Light Opera Company" is a colorful look at the role of Cape Cod's theater boot camp in training the next generation of actors.

Thanks to all the executive and artistic directors and board members at all the theater companies on Cape Cod and the Islands for taking the time to tell me the stories of their theaters. It is their collective wisdom and experience that you see reflected on every page of this book. Special thanks to David Drake, artistic director of The Provincetown Theater, who shared a wealth of information about the early artists in Provincetown.

And a special thanks to past theater artists' family members who were willing to meet with me and share memories about their parents' theater worlds and their early memories of childhoods in the footlights.

Thanks to Michael and Suz Karchmer, who contributed a number of their wonderful photos to the book.

And, finally, thanks to Kathi Scrizzi Driscoll, who kindly consented to write the foreword to this book. And more than that, thanks for making this book possible by having the faith to take me back into the fold after such a lengthy absence.

Additional resources that proved invaluable:

Provincetown History Preservation Project

Building Provincetown: The History of Provincetown Told through Its Built Environment, written and photographed by David W. Dunlap.

The website I Am Provincetown, written and maintained by artist Ewa Nogiec, with contributions from numerous locals.

1

SUN, SURF AND SPOTLIGHTS

THE ENDURING WORLD OF THEATER ON CAPE COD

I t's a summer's eve on Cape Cod, and up and down the peninsula waves lap steadily against the shore, gulls cry out and children laugh and chatter as they play a never-ending game of tag with the waves and one another. These are the age-old sounds of summer on Olde Cape Cod. (And, okay, let's face it, there is the modern addition of car engines and horns competing with the sounds of nature for airtime.)

But everywhere up and down and across the Cape are also other sounds that waft through the air throughout the summer season and, increasingly, all year long. These are the soaring sounds of orchestras tuning up for an overture, laughter at flawlessly performed physical comedy, dramatic lines cutting through the air like razor-sharp knives and—everywhere—applause, applause, applause. And here's maybe the best part: There are no TVs or movie screens involved. These are the sounds of the more than three dozen theater companies that dot Cape Cod and the Islands, as they continue to build the lively, vibrant culture of live theater on the Cape.

A TOUCH OF NEW YORK ON THE DUNES

This may be the best thing about theater on Cape Cod: The theater-going public and critics alike generally agree that it just keeps getting better and better. In fact, theater buffs across the region have come to expect a level of performance expertise usually available only in metropolitan theater

Cape Cod, the home of summer fun and great theater. *GoodPhotos*.

centers like New York and San Francisco. All summer long—and in recent years into the off-season—vacationers trek literally from all over the world for a little sun, sand and Sondheim. They know that if they want New York–quality theater without the noise, congestion and gritty summer heat of the city, they will find it in one of the often-historic theaters on Cape Cod. In fact, according to the Cape and Islands Theatre Coalition, which helps keep the public informed of the region's diverse dramatic offerings, more than six hundred thousand people attend performances on the Cape and Islands every year.

There are myriad theories about why the Cape has become such a bastion of live theater. Certainly, the sheer power of competition is a major factor. Theater companies—which number upward of thirty on the peninsula at this printing—are all too well aware that on any given summer night theater-lovers have almost endless choices when it comes to the dramatic arts. In the mood for a popular musical filled with young, athletic dancers leaping across the stage? You can find it all year long at the Cape Cod Theatre Company in Harwich or at the Highfield Theatre in Falmouth, where the College Light Opera Company takes to the stage in the summer months and the Falmouth Theatre Guild takes over the venue in the off-season.

If, on the other hand, you'd like something a little more serious and thought-provoking to hit the restart button in your prefrontal lobe, there are likely to be any number of choices at the tip of the Cape, including a Eugene O'Neill play offered by either the Provincetown Theater or Provincetown Dramatic Arts. (How about this for drama: In one recent Dramatic Arts production of the O'Neill play *Anna Christie*, the massive wooden doors on the wharf theater were opened onto the harbor. Throughout the play, the sea became a living, breathing and omniscient presence. Interestingly, the sea actually made its first appearance as a lead character in the very first staging of O'Neill's very first play, *Bound East for Cardiff*, which actually marked the very beginning of American drama as we know it. Of course, no discussion of theater on Cape Cod would be complete without a thorough look at the influence of O'Neill and his contemporaries. I'll offer that look in chapter 2 and at various junctures throughout the book.)

Your search for drama might also take you the short distance to the Wellfleet Harbor Actors Theater for a work by a new playwright in the Julie Harris Theater. Or you could travel a little farther up-Cape to the Bayside town of Brewster, where the Cape Cod Repertory Theatre works with professional actors and playwrights to further the group's commitment to

Cape Cod Theatre Company/Home of the Harwich Junior Theatre, *Beauty and the Beast*, 2018. *Cape Cod Theatre Company Staff.*

"telling great stories." And if you're up for a little trip across Nantucket Sound, you might catch an original work at the Theatre Workshop of Nantucket, where professional actors often hailing from the Great White Way join with talented locals to produce works that keep alive a thriving island tradition of theater. And, if you happen to be stretching the season into late September and feel like circling back to the tip of the Cape—and to the very beginnings of American drama—you might want to catch a day or two of the Tennessee Williams Festival. There you can catch one of Williams's works, along with some newer works in the Williams tradition, along with some innovative performance art.

In the mood for a little star power? It's there at the Cape Playhouse in Dennis, the oldest professional summer playhouse in the country at ninety-three at this writing. An almost endless list of Hollywood and Broadway luminaries—including the likes of Gertrude Lawrence, Julie Andrews and Julie Harris—have spent large chunks of summer seasons there. (In Lawrence's case, the playhouse literally became home. More on that later.) And every season, the playhouse brings in Tony Award–winning talent to continually feed aficionados' continuing hunger for star power.

And just a couple of towns over in Hyannis is the Melody Tent, which began life as a dramatic arts venue and has evolved into a site for musical entertainment, with a steady stream of noted performers gracing its stage for decades. (One Melody Tent legend says that Bonnie Raitt cut her musical teeth there tagging along with her musical-comedy-star dad, John.) Or you can take another trip toward the tip of the Cape and find stars at the Payomet Arts Center in Truro, which offers a mixed bag of live

Drawing of the Cape Playhouse. *Author's collection.*

music, theater and—wait for it—a Cirque du Soleil–style circus experience. Musical performers at Payomet have recently included cultural icons like Arlo Guthrie, Mary Chapin Carpenter and Taj Mahal.

Bottom line: Fierce competition virtually defines the theater and live entertainment experience on Cape Cod. But there's something more: there's a tradition, a dedication to theater that extends from Provincetown to Falmouth and the Islands and envelops performers and audiences alike. And, maybe more important, literally thousands of actors, directors and technicians feed the well-nourished cultural industry that is Cape Cod theater. Obviously, this virtual obsession had to begin somewhere—and so it did. It began in what was once a quiet little fishing village at the tip of the Cape that became a thriving artists' colony and to this day is a mecca for writers, visual artists and, of course, playwrights and performers.

So, let's begin at the beginning—at the land's end.

And Then There Is the History

In the late nineteenth and early twentieth centuries, there was a virtual revolution going on in every area of the arts. Authors like Henry David Thoreau and Henry James and artists like James Whistler in the United States and, of course, Pablo Picasso, Édouard Manet and Claude Monet in Europe, were breaking new artistic ground. In keeping with that revolutionary environment, the genesis of Provincetown (and eventually Cape Cod) as an art colony has its roots in the establishment of the Cape Cod School of Art in 1899 by impressionist painter Charles Webster Hawthorne. As authors of the site I Am Provincetown note, aspiring artists came to his school to learn en plein air, which, as its name implies, focuses on creating works outdoors.

Soon, dozens of artists, writers and playwrights were taking the new railway line to Provincetown to join their revolutionary brothers and sisters. It only seems natural that artists of every kind would come to this spot literally at the end (or beginning) of the Earth to leap into new and uncharted territory.

By the second decade of the new century, expatriates who had traded American soil for the salons and cafés of Europe were fleeing the war on the continent and joining their comrades in artist colonies like Greenwich Village and Provincetown. In fact, the colony became so popular that in 1916 the *Boston Globe* printed the headline "Biggest Art Colony in the World at Provincetown." Artists and writers who lived and worked in New York and Boston in the winter hopped a train for the Cape and wended their way on

PROVINCETOWN PLAYHOUSE

WHARF OFF GOSNOLD ST.

SEASON'S LAST PRODUCTION
EUGENE O'NEILL'S

"THE EMPEROR JONES"

MON. AUG. 30 - MON. SEPT. 6 LABOR DAY

Special Performance Sunday Sept. 5th - Actor's Benefit

EVERY EVENING AT 8:30

Tickets $1.10, $1.64, $2.40 (tax included)   Tel. 26-M

Poster for the Eugene O'Neill play *The Emperor Jones. Courtesy of Pilgrim Monument and Provincetown Museum.*

to Provincetown to create masterpieces amid the dunes. Revolutionaries—both in terms of their art and politics—like Jack Reed and Louise Bryant were among that group. Also among the first settlers of the Provincetown Art Colony were playwrights Susan Glaspell and Eugene O'Neill. Glaspell was responsible for convincing many fellow artists to help her build the new way of life on the Cape. And O'Neill was responsible for, without exaggeration, giving birth to the American theater as we know it today. With a little one-act play first staged in Provincetown, *Bound East for Cardiff*, and other works that followed, he led the art away from European-style performance to a new, truly American art form.

And that, logically enough, is where the story begins. I'll revisit the beginnings of American (and Cape Cod) theater, then guide the reader through a tour of the land of Mediterranean light and its theater history.

It's curtain time.

2

PROVINCETOWN

AT THE LAND'S END IS THE BEGINNING

By the second decade of the twentieth century, Provincetown had become a virtual outpost for artists and intellectuals from Greenwich Village. Artists were everywhere—on the beaches, dunes and town streets—working to capture the beauty of the world bathed in the unique Cape Cod light. Among them were several writers and playwrights who were disillusioned by the stodginess and commercialism of Broadway. Until that point, American theater was merely an extension of classical European theater—with a little cheap melodrama and vaudeville thrown in for good measure.

The revolutionaries in Provincetown wanted to smash the classical European mold and create something brand new, something that would appeal to "the fishermen who were paying 50 cents a seat," rather than the well-fed audiences on Broadway, says David Drake, current artistic director of the Provincetown Theater. "They wanted to know what their own pens could do."

So, in the summer of 1915, a group that included Susan Glaspell (who would go on to win a Pulitzer for drama), and her husband, George "Jig" Cram Cook, and Neith Boyce and her husband, Hutchins Hapgood, staged an evening of one-act plays at Boyce's home. The plays *Suppressed Desires* by Glaspell and Cook and *Constancy* by Boyce were both witty spoofs and well received among the intellectuals and artists who themselves had come to the end of the world for just this kind of intellectual revolution. Drake points out that the democratic nature of the group extended to their productions; the group took turns producing scripts and acting in one another's plays.

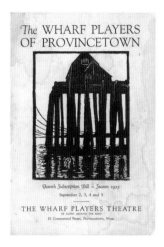

The WHARF PLAYERS
OF PROVINCETOWN

Fourth Subscription Bill ~ Season 1925
September 2, 3, 4 and 5

THE WHARF PLAYERS THEATRE
OF ALONG AROUND THE BEND
83 Commercial Street, Provincetown, Mass.

Playbill from Wharf Theatre.
Courtesy of Pilgrim Monument and Provincetown Museum.

So the group planned another staging of the plays, this time in an old fish house on Lewis Wharf in Provincetown's East End, offered to the group by Mary Heaton Vorse, a journalist, novelist, social critic and activist who maintained lifelong ties to the art community on the tip of the Cape. In fact, she—along with Glaspell and other artists/activists including Jack Reed and Louise Bryant—were among the first to put down roots in Ptown. In the early years of the colony, Vorse was influential in convincing many of her fellow artists to trade the confines of New York for the freedom of Cape Cod. Fittingly, she died in her home in Provincetown in 1966 at the age of ninety-two. Her book *Time and the Town* is still a Bible for Ptown lovers.

Throughout the winter of 1915–16, enthusiasm remained high and a second season was planned for the old wharf building—which was now outfitted with a makeshift theater. It's interesting to note that, in a campaign piece designed to garner income through subscriptions, Cook noted that the aim of the group was "to give American playwrights a chance to work out their ideas in freedom." He couldn't possibly have known just how prophetic that statement was to become.

The Moment True American Theater Was Born

Clearly, playwrights like Glaspell and Cook and the small vanguard of revolutionaries in Provincetown had begun to lay the fertile ground where American drama as an art form could take root and flourish. They were determined to create an entirely new category that—like the work of the visual artists who surrounded them—focused on realism. But many theater historians point to one single event—the staging of Eugene O'Neill's *Bound East for Cardiff* on July 28, 1916, in the little theater on Lewis Wharf—as the beginning of theater as a uniquely American construct.

The young playwright's somewhat inauspicious entrance on the Provincetown art scene was as a sailor on a boat that came in from Boston. He was, in fact, no stranger to life at sea, having recently worked his way

Eugene O'Neill (*right*) and artist Charles Demuth (*left*). *Courtesy Dr. Jeffrey Kennedy and the New England Historical Society.*

northward from Buenos Aires on a steamer. And that first summer he was often seen around town shirtless in shorts or swimsuits. (It's been said that Henry David Thoreau—who, back in 1849, walked the thirty miles of uninterrupted Atlantic coast along Cape Cod and later wrote about the experience—wanted simply to look at the sea, while O'Neill wanted to be part of it.)

But if the sea was in his blood, so was theater. His father was the successful actor and theater entrepreneur James O'Neill, so Eugene had spent a good part of his life around actors and playwrights. Soon after making his landfall in Provincetown, O'Neill sought out the group of bohemians he knew were producing groundbreaking work in Provincetown. Susan Glaspell was one of the first to meet him, and she subsequently championed his work with the group. Not that much promotion was necessary; it is said that, as soon as the group read *Bound East*, they knew it was the springboard that would propel fledgling American drama forward. They suddenly knew why they had come together in the first place. While it reflected some of the somber mood of European playwrights like Ibsen and Strindberg, its characters were uniquely American (the lead character's name is Yank) and its emphasis on the struggles of the lower classes would become a lynchpin of American drama. Some critics have said this was the first time that emotions that had previously been limited to novels and poems found their way to the American stage.

The group unanimously decided to stage *Bound East* and did so in a matter of days, with O'Neill co-directing and taking on a minor role. Accounts of opening night from contemporaries like Vorse paint a scene of fog thickening around groups of theater-goers that included the likes of revolutionaries Louise Bryant, Jack Reed and Max Eastman and artists Charles Dermuth and Marsden Hartley. Inside, the building's massive, story-high doors were opened onto the harbor, making the sea and sky a constant, godlike presence in the production and helping to set the scene of a stalled tramp steamer on the Atlantic. (O'Neill often remarked that it seemed natural for the sea to play such a major part in his first production, since it had always been a part of his life. And theater legend has it that O'Neill was also ever-present, as he crouched in the wings and voiced prompts to the actors, who'd had only a few days to rehearse.)

Despite the lack of rehearsal time, the show was a great success; historical accounts note that the old and rotting fish house/theater literally shook with the force of the applause that night. It seems more than appropriate that arguably the most important night in the history of American theater should

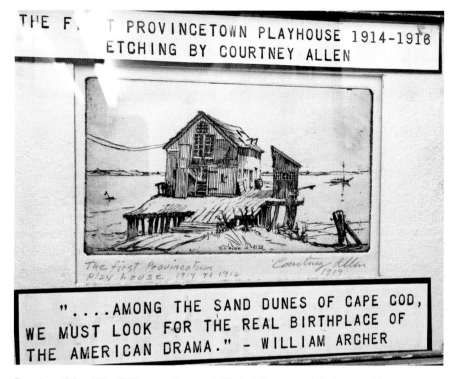

THE F. T PROVINCETOWN PLAYHOUSE 1914-1916
ETCHING BY COURTNEY ALLEN

"....AMONG THE SAND DUNES OF CAPE COD,
WE MUST LOOK FOR THE REAL BIRTHPLACE OF
THE AMERICAN DRAMA." - WILLIAM ARCHER

Drawing of first Wharf Theatre. *Courtesy of Pilgrim Monument and Provincetown Museum.*

be greeted with thunderous applause. According to writer A.J. Philpott, writing in the *Boston Post* on August 13, 1916, the play was "a gripping thing—shows how easily death comes into most men's lives, and how they treat it." And Vorse later said that "it has never been played more authentically than it was by our group of amateurs…with the sound of the sea beneath it."

A Wellspring of Creativity Bursts Forth

Clearly, the American theater movement was poised and ready to move forward from that moment at the first Playhouse on the Wharf, and so it did. In the fall of 1916, the group, led by Cook and Reed, formally adopted the name The Provincetown Players and voted to stage a season of plays in New York. So they made their way back to the city, where they rented a theater they named The Playwright's Theatre.

As it turned out, the group spent a lot longer than one season producing plays in Gotham. Through the next seven years, in both The

Vintage programs, Wharf Theatre. *Courtesy of Pilgrim Monument and Provincetown Museum.*

Playwright's Theatre and its successor, The Provincetown Playhouse, the group produced a list of works by such greats as Glaspell, Edna St. Vincent Millay and, of course, O'Neill. The 1920–21 season spotlighted O'Neill's *The Emperor Jones*, which was an instant and stunning success. The production featured Charles Gilpin, the first African American professional actor to perform with a white company, and an innovative set design centered on a dome that was fitted into the theater. In the next season, the group produced O'Neill's *The Hairy Ape*, which had commercial backing—a first for the group.

As is all too often the case, commercial success ate away the bonds among group members, and by 1923, the active members voted to disband. In 1922, before he and Glaspell left for a trip to Greece, Cook presaged the group's demise, writing that they had given "the theater we had loved a good death."

As Drake notes, "That original group performed as amateurs so they were free to experiment. It was that determination that actually led to the birth of experimental American theater."

Back at Land's End

The original Playhouse on the Wharf burned in 1917 and disappeared into the sea in 1922. At that point, activity moved to the west end of town, where one of the original Provincetown Players, an editor and bookseller named Frank Shay, converted his barn into a playhouse and named it the Barnstormers' Theater. Shay, who had operated a bookstore in Greenwich Village that was a center of the village's bohemian lifestyle, had started making his way to Ptown—with a carful of books to sell and an abiding interest in theater—for summers in 1921. In 1924, he and his wife, Fern, permanently moved to the town. (Shay eventually wrote a book titled *The Practical Theatre: A Manual for Little Theatres, Community Players, Amateur Dramatic Clubs and Other Independent Producing Groups.*)

While at this point the pioneers from the Players, including O'Neill, Vorse and Harry Kemp, spent large chunks of the year in New York, they still gravitated back to the tip of the Cape and continued writing for and performing in Barnstormers' productions.

The second iteration of the Playhouse on the Wharf was born in 1923. Initially, the group, headed by actress Mary Bicknell, performed in a movie theater. Then Bicknell and her troupe joined forces with Frank Shay's Barnstormers. But all was not well in the hayloft; Bicknell and her group were traditionalists and disagreed with the avant-garde bent in the Barnstormers' productions. In fact, according to local theater legend, the relationship got so heated that the Bicknell group absconded with props, equipment and audience benches. Predictably, the group built its own theater, which came to be known as the Wharf Players Theater, in 1925, on what had been known as the Myrick Atwood Wharf, at 83 Commercial Street.

For the first couple of years, the new Theatre on the Wharf seemed destined for success. But then Bicknell—who tired of the financial strain of making the theater work—abandoned the group. Successive managers never seemed to find the right formula to make the theater a going concern. Mercifully, you might say, the building fell into the sea during a fierce storm in 1940.

The BARNSTORMERS
of PROVINCETOWN
in
"S. S. GLENCAIRN"
Four Episodes of the Sea
By EUGENE O'NEILL

At the Barnstormers' Barn
PROVINCETOWN
Aug. 14, 15, 16, 18, 19, 1924
Matinee Saturday August 16

Barnstormers program.
Provincetown Historic Preservation Project. Stand-alone Documents.

Once again, the sea had carried away the town's only serious theater (by that time, the Barnstormers had also petered out). But a very Cape Cod–ish solution was on the way. A well-known local artist named Heinrich Pfeiffer had a vision that was way ahead of his time. It all began when he started operating art classes in a building on a wharf in the center of town at the foot of Gosnold Street owned by boatbuilder Jonathan Small. (Interestingly, Small also built sandwiches at his restaurant called "Jot's.") It would appear that Jot and partner Ross Moffett were better artists than painters, because the school lasted only one season. Still, Pfeiffer bought the wharf from Small and gave the place the very appropriate name Art Colony Wharf. He had built a small, two-hundred-seat theater in the hope of convincing moviegoers to add avant-garde films to a diet of slick and sugary extravaganzas Hollywood was churning out. The Artists' Theatre opened in 1937 and began showing a combination of foreign and underground films, with a smattering of live theater mixed in. Pfeiffer eventually realized that moviegoers were addicted to their celluloid junk food, so he went in search of a group of players that could bring live theater into the town again, to once again present "the kind of plays which made Provincetown famous in the days of Eugene O'Neill and Susan Glaspell." He found that group in the New England Repertory Company of Boston.

As it turned out, founding members of the group—director Edward Burr Pettet, actor and publicity director Catharine Huntington and actor and costume designer Virginia Thoms—were enthralled with O'Neill and Glaspell and determined to give their work a rebirth at the tip of the Cape. As is all too often the case with community theaters, the group had to wade through some financial snafus, but thanks to some timely community backing they were able to purchase the theater and wharf from Pfeiffer. At first, the group operated under the name The Artists' Theatre, but change was on the way.

The group soon took the name the Provincetown Playhouse (not to be confused with the Provincetown Playhouse in Greenwich Village, home of the original Provincetown Players) and delivered in spades on its promise to feature works by O'Neill and Glaspell. After closing during World War II, the playhouse opened with *Anna Christie*, O'Neill's brilliant work about life on the waterfront and a young woman desperately struggling to save herself from drowning (figuratively speaking). Every year, in fact, Huntington and company started the season with an O'Neill piece, then followed up with works by the likes of Edward Albee, Glaspell, Tennessee Williams, George Bernard Shaw and Harry Kemp. (Here's a little bit of Provincetown history: Huntington performed for the last time in 1969 in Williams's *Camino Real* along with Richard Gere at the Playhouse. Another notable tidbit: Town theater history says Gere and Williams roomed together for a time.)

By the beginning of the 1970s, Huntington and company had tired of the financial strain of the theater, so in 1972 they sold the property to Lester and Adele Heller, longtime summer residents and members of the local arts community. Adele had been publicity director of Act IV Café Experimental Theatre, a quirky little group that had briefly basked in the limelight in the 1960s. (More on that group momentarily.) The Hellers continued to stage the works of Provincetown greats, including O'Neill and Williams, along with works by new, avant-garde playwrights such as Harold Pinter. (A note about one Williams play, *The Night of the Iguana:* According to the Hellers' daughter artist Amy Heller, the group actually used a live iguana in the show, which it housed on the theater's second floor.) And the Hellers maintained an apprenticeship program, with a number of apprentices gaining Equity status.

Unfortunately, just a few years later, in 1977, the Playhouse was destroyed by arson. (The story goes that a group of local teenagers who were denied liquor at a watering hole, the Crown & Anchor, set fire to cushions in the theater. Most of the theater was engulfed, and forty-year-old costumes and artifacts were destroyed.)

Following the tragedy, various plans were floated for an expansive arts complex on the wharf, including the possibility of bringing in government funding to purchase additional space for an expansive complex. In fact, Adele Heller was able to secure a grant from the National Endowment for the Arts for a design competition for a new space, with famed architect I.M. Pei serving as a judge and Helen Hayes as master of ceremonies. But funding never materialized, so the project didn't move forward. But the Hellers continued for the next several years to produce plays and musical events in spaces around town, including the town hall. And Lester turned the box office—which managed to escape the flames in 1977—into the Eugene O'Neill Theatre Museum, where he displayed a slide show about the history of theater in the town. Daughter and Provincetown art dealer/collector and gallerist Julie Heller—who still uses the old box office for gallery space—says her parents were "dedicated to the arts throughout their lives. They were true renaissance people." She notes that, through the rest of her life, her mother continued to support and volunteer for groups around town. And, in true renaissance fashion, Adele also penned a book titled *1915, The Cultural Moment* and edited Mary Heaton Vorse's Provincetown favorite, *Time and the Town.* And, not surprisingly, she was made a member of the esteemed Eugene O'Neill Society.

Not the Final Act

While the Playhouse drama was moving toward its tragic conclusion, other groups in town were evolving and continuing to thrive. (Perhaps the most notable survivor is the group that became The Provincetown Theater. A full chronology is to come.)

One group that stands as an interesting sidebar in the Provincetown theater story was Act IV Café Experimental Theatre, which initially took up space in the basement of the 150-year-old Gifford House Inn, then moved to the Weathering Heights Club on Shank Painter Road. The big news here is that the group just happened to have the support of Cape and theater aficionado Norman Mailer. The midcentury master of letters and wife Beverly Bentley were involved with the theater periodically through its four-season existence, from 1966 to 1969.

The theater was the brainchild of a triumvirate of notables—Robert Costa, Doug Ross and Eric Krebs—who, from the group's beginnings, were determined to live up to their name. Costa, the group's artistic director, says it was a time when "the whole discipline of experimental theater was taking off, and we were a part of that." In the course of four seasons "underground," Act IV staged an unprecedented roster of new and edgy works, including a piece by Israel Horovitz, *The Indian Wants the Bronx*, which just happened to star the newly minted actor Al Pacino. Pacino shared the stage with John Cazale, who would go on to play Fredo Corleone in *The Godfather* and *The Godfather: Part II*. The group also showed "underground" movies and staged some children's productions.

Then there were the Mailers. In the first season, the group produced Norman Mailer's *The Deer Park*, based on his novel. It went on to the Theatre de Lys in Greenwich Village, with Bentley performing in both versions. Other soon-to-be-famous performers who stepped on the Act IV stage included Jerry Stiller and Anne Meara, Jill Clayburgh and Sally Kirkland.

By 1969, the Act IV story had reached its final curtain. But here's the thing about the theater culture in Provincetown: Neither arson nor closing acts of individual theaters mean that theater in general—and the O'Neill tradition—die at Land's End. After all, the tradition is just too compelling. This is the place where O'Neill wrote *Emperor Jones* and *The Hairy Ape* and Tennessee Williams finished *The Glass Menagerie*. In fact, this little spit of land with a year-round population of just three thousand boasts seven Pulitzer winners. Along with O'Neill, Williams and Glaspell, the list includes Norman Mailer, William Cunningham, Stanley Kunitz and Mary Oliver.

Survivors

Theater groups now carrying on the tradition in Provincetown include the Provincetown Theater, the Peregrine Theatre Ensemble and Provincetown Dramatic Arts.

The Provincetown Theater/New Provincetown Players opened its doors for the first time in 1963, in its original incarnation as the Provincetown Theatre Workshop. From the start, the company was a mix of professional, semiprofessional and talented nonprofessional local actors, writers, musicians, artists, directors and technicians. The group emphasized a mixture of staged readings, original plays by local writers and works by established playwrights—a combination that has continued to be the focus of the company. In a way, its very diversity and dedication to the arts and theater community in Ptown make it the theatrical descendant of the early wharf theaters and the Provincetown Players.

According to the history section of the theater's website (www. provincetowntheater.org) from 1963 through 1972, the company lived a gypsy's existence, moving from space to space, but still managed to mount more and more ambitious productions. In the winter of 1973, the Provincetown Theatre Workshop was renamed the Provincetown Theatre Company and The Provincetown Academy of Performing Arts and Museum.

In 1988–89, the company moved to the Provincetown Inn, meaning the group had performing space for plays, revues and staged readings. That gave the company the impetus to enter into an artistic collaboration with acclaimed artist and playwright Edward Gorey. During this period, the company produced three of his plays.

In 1993, with the loss of the performing space at the Inn, the group's future looked bleak. But by 1996, the group's board had re-dedicated itself to community theater in the town, and ties were re-established with the Provincetown Inn, where the company continued to perform until it merged with the Provincetown Repertory Theatre (REP) in 2006. In addition to a year-round season, the company produces a highly successful playwriting competition that annually celebrates the work of a Massachusetts playwright with a cash award and a staged reading of his/her work. According to artistic director David Drake, "We'd like to think we have nourished the ambitions of many people interested in pursuing a career in the theater."

And Drake points to the fact that theater education has spread up and across the Cape, with groups like the Academy of Performing Arts in Orleans and the Cape Cod Theatre Company in Harwich training dozens of young people every year. These theater apprentices then go on and add to the always-growing community of performers and playwrights that crisscrosses Cape Cod. (More on this later.)

The Provincetown Repertory Theatre was founded in 1995 as a professional, Equity company. Its goal was to produce a mix of works historically linked to Provincetown, new plays and contemporary classics to entertain and engage Cape Cod audiences. Paula Vogel's *The Mineola Twins* and the musical *Amphigorey*, based on Cape resident Edward Gorey's book of the same name, are two examples. Both Vogel and Gorey had their world premieres at the REP before heading off to New York City productions, continuing the Provincetown tradition as an important place for the development of new American work by great American writers, including the likes of Edward Albee and Terrence McNally. But the company also spotlighted the works of O'Neill, Williams and Lillian Hellman.

PTC and the Provincetown Repertory Theatre began discussions to consolidate staff and merge in October 2005. This became a reality on January 1, 2006, when the combined theater company became known as the New Provincetown Players and assumed both ownership and operations of the Provincetown Theater.

It was thanks to the work of the **Provincetown Theater Foundation**, established in 2001, that the community where American drama was born now has a permanent home for an important part of its theater community, at 238 Bradford Street in Provincetown. The foundation raised funds from a wide variety of local contributors to purchase what had once been an auto-repair garage and construct a state-of-the-art theater in the heart of the city.

(Anyone who thought the 1977 fire on the wharf dealt a fatal blow to theater in Provincetown underestimated the community's commitment to and love of live theater. These days, the resident company produces shows ranging from local playwrights' works to Broadway classics like *Sweeney Todd, The Demon Barber of Fleet Street* and holiday favorites like *It's a Wonderful Life: A Live Radio Play.*)

The Peregrine Theatre Ensemble actually derives its name from Peregrine White, the first child born to the Pilgrims in the New World while the *Mayflower* was anchored in Provincetown Harbor. Group members like to say that their group "embodies that same adventure and passion of braving uncharted possibilities."

Peregrine Theatre Ensemble is, in fact, another group dedicated not just to performance but also to ensuring that the arts survive in Provincetown and the wider world for generations to come. In fact, each season, the

Peregrine Theatre Company, 2018 production of *Hair*. *Michael and Suz Karchmer.*

company is composed of professional student actors, production members and musicians who join the group to explore and develop their craft. So the company sponsors a range of performances and workshops, and joins with other nonprofit organizations, resulting in increased sustainability for the Provincetown community.

Provincetown Dramatic Arts is another company currently on the Provincetown theater scene. In 2004, the company, composed of both professionals and amateur actors, was founded by Margaret Van Sant, who has been a part of the Cape Cod theater community since the 1960s, when she did "exciting work" with the Provincetown Theater. At the time, the company was experimenting with nontraditional casting—casting men in women's roles and vice versa. She then established a theater company in Northampton, where she and "a talented group of people" produced a number of American premieres, did Shakespeare in the park and introduced a number of new playwrights, eventually returning to her theater roots on Cape Cod. (As Drake points out, "everyone eventually washes back ashore on Cape Cod.")

Introducing and supporting new playwrights has been a theme of the company since its inception, with its annual Women's Festival the perfect example. Each spring, the company sponsors a festival featuring the work of women playwrights from all over the Cape, with women from major metropolitan markets also making the trek to the lower Cape for the event. Women are encouraged not only to spotlight their own work but also to direct plays at the festival.

And the group also annually takes plays to the Dublin International Gay Theatre Festival, where, Van Sant says, "It's absolutely soul-satisfying to be with people from all over the world, focusing on great theater. It's all too easy sometimes to get caught up in your own little world and the things you're doing. That can be especially true in a place like Cape Cod, which is actually physically cut off; it's easy to get a little insular in your approach."

But it's almost impossible to exist as a theater company in Provincetown and not be tinged in the colors of the early Players and especially O'Neill. Van Sant talks about "celebrating the rich cultural heritage of the community," with productions like *Anna Christie*, which the group featured in both its 2016 and 2017 seasons. In a reenactment of the staging one hundred years before of O'Neill's *Bound East for Cardiff*, the group performed in an old wharf building on the Provincetown waterfront, its massive doors opened up to the sea and sky, making the watery world the overwhelming presence O'Neill always intended. And the group intends to continue to offer O'Neill plays, along with more modern works. In recent years, for example, PDA has presented *Venus in Fur* by David Ives and *The Tale of the Allergist's Wife* by Charles Busch.

Van Sant says that, in a place like Provincetown, with its expansive community dedicated to the theater arts, it seems appropriate that the initials of her group (PDA) can also be understood to mean "public displays of affection"—in this case, for the dramatic arts.

One contemporary group that has formed with the specific aim of keeping Provincetown theater history alive is the **Heritage Theatre of Provincetown**, inaugurated in September 2019. And artistic director Stuard Derrick is determined to be sure that what survives is a true reflection of the town's theater history.

"There's a lot of incorrect or incomplete information around," he says. "We want to be sure the right information gets out there."

The group, he says, is dedicated to "preserving and reviving" works that were associated with past groups, especially groups like the original Provincetown Players and the Barnstormers. "We want to prove these [plays] are not creaky old things. They are still playable." To that end, the group's 2020 summer season will spotlight a world premiere of *The Sea Lady* by Neith Boyce, one of the founding members of the original Provincetown Players.

Derrick has worked with Boyce expert Catherine DeBoer Langworthy to ensure that the production is a true interpretation of Boyce's original work, which is based on the H.G. Wells novel of the same name. At this printing, the premiere is slated to be performed on June 7, 2020, at the Pilgrim Monument and Provincetown Museum as part of the museum's celebration of the four-hundredth anniversary of the Pilgrims' landing. The group is also planning monthly readings of early works in various venues around Ptown. And in a series titled "Reclaimed Voices," the group will present works by artists who were lost in the AIDS epidemic.

Finally, Derrick says he wants to go way back in theater history, making Shakespearean theater a regular part of the scene in Provincetown. "We want to do whatever we can to make Provincetown a true destination for theater people everywhere," he says.

The Tennessee Williams Festival

And then there is the continuing tradition of a festival dedicated to the work of one of Provincetown's greats: Tennessee Williams. Ever since 2007, for four days in the last week in September, Provincetown has turned its attention to the work and dramatic legacy of its famous former resident. Williams, according to theater history, finished his play *The Glass Menagerie* at a little rooming house in Provincetown. In fact, he actually worked on a number of his major works in the town in the 1940s. The Tennessee Williams Festival, first organized in Provincetown in 2006, literally turns the town into a stage that week, performing Williams and Williams-inspired works in venues all over town.

Every year, Cape Codders and Williams aficionados from as far away as the United Kingdom and California come to be literally bathed in the work of Williams, as the festival takes over every likely venue—and some not so likely. The troupe has been known to use cafés, hotel rooms and swimming pools to tell its stories.

There could hardly be a better place for the festival—which now travels all over the country—to call home. Provincetown's long theater history and the continuing vibrancy of its artistic community means that its audiences are uniquely sophisticated and open to new and groundbreaking approaches to theater. And festival fans, says curator David Kaplan, are a global community of theater-goers who communicate throughout the year, then reconnect in Provincetown to sample the fare late in September.

In his book *Tennessee Williams in Provincetown*, Kaplan spins the tale of Williams's relationship with the seaside village. And he offers on the festival website (www.twptown.org) this condensed version of the history and the festival's role in perpetuating that history.

> *"I am moving into a little shanty in the dunes where I can avoid the summer crowds. I find this is a good place to work and think I will get a play off to you next week."*—*Tennessee Williams in a 1944 letter from Provincetown to agent Audrey Wood*
>
> *On the edge, artistically and geographically, Provincetown prides itself on embracing creativity and diversity and attracting legendary artists, writers and filmmakers to its protected and pristine environment.*
>
> *As America's great playwright Tennessee Williams was influenced in his work and his personal life by the spirit and openness of Provincetown, it is fitting that the Provincetown Tennessee Williams Theater Festival celebrate Williams with the same spirit of discovery—of one's self and of the world—that he tapped in this small town.*
>
> *Over several summers during the 1940s, Tennessee Williams worked in a shack on the dunes or on a wharf in the bay and crafted many of his masterful works, including* The Glass Menagerie *and* A Streetcar Named Desire.
>
> *Provincetown was also significant in Tennessee's personal life as this is where he fell in love for the first time and where he later met the man with whom he would have a deep and abiding fourteen-year relationship.*
>
> *The aim of the TW Festival is to keep the spirit of Tennessee Williams alive and inspire new generations through its performance and exploration of his early work, mature masterpieces, and experimental plays.*

(Here's an interesting historical tidbit that once again emphasizes the importance of Provincetown in entertainment history. After reading *A Streetcar Named Desire*, Marlon Brando is said to have hitchhiked to Ptown to cajole Williams to give him the role as Stanley Kowalski. And the rest is, as they say, theater and film history.)

Writing in *American Theater Magazine*, critic Randy Gener wrote about the importance of the festival to American drama. "Williams is a giant—prescient, pitiless and well-nigh impregnable....By giving us Williams unplugged, the brave folks at the Provincetown festival are doing the necessary, good work, outside the confines of commercial bottom feeding.... Williams's dramaturgy is still ahead of our time."

And, according to Kaplan, the festival is about more than simply perpetuating the history of Williams; it's actually about expanding the Williams universe to include the whole range of other artists, works and themes that are somehow related to his work. So, every year, festival productions revolve around a central theme, with that theme being interpreted through drama, music, dance and performance art.

For example, in 2018, the festival focused on waiting, or "the drama of anticipation," by bringing together Williams plays, including *The Rose Tattoo* and a world premiere of *Talisman Roses*, with pieces by Federico García Lorca, Anton Chekhov and Samuel Beckett, all focusing on the central theme. The season also featured the motif of roses, with Lorca's *Doña Rosita the Spinster* appearing alongside Williams's rose-related pieces.

Tennessee Williams. New York Telegram and Sun *Collection, Library of Congress.*

In an unusual—and perhaps unprecedented—move, in 2017, the festival reached way back in theater history to pair Williams's work with those by Shakespeare. So, for instance, the Bard's plays *Hamlet* and *Antony and Cleopatra* were performed along with Williams's plays *Sweet Bird of Youth* and *Ten Blocks on the Camino Real*. And the week included social events and educational programming that drove home the direct line between Shakespeare and Williams. By the end of the week, audiences became adept at drawing comparisons between the two masters.

It's also important to note that the festival takes its productions not just on the road but also to the clouds, now traveling globally with some of Williams's lesser-known plays hitting the boards in the United States and beyond. According to Kaplan: "It is our mission to see that Tennessee Williams is fully understood for the creative force that he was, and that goes well beyond his classic masterpieces. Williams was always writing and experimenting and much of his work was dismissed in his time. Our performances offer exciting and pioneering approaches to his work that turn plays thought impossible to stage or to understand into theatrical excitement that audiences everywhere embrace."

The group hopes that Tennessee Williams's reputation is being revitalized as more audiences and critics are seeing "the full breadth and vitality of the full range of Williams' work in performance," notes Kaplan.

Since beginning in 2007, several productions festival audiences saw first at the tip of Cape Cod, as well as variations on them, have continued to spread out into the world, revitalizing the reputation of the great American playwright for his creative accomplishments, Kaplan says.

In just the 2015–16 season, for example, among other productions, the troupe took *Orpheus Descending* to New York and New Orleans, *The Remarkable Rooming-House of Mme. LeMonde* to New York and Boston, *The Rooming House Plays* to St. Louis and—in partnership with Abrahamse-Meyer Productions—*The Day on Which a Man Dies* to South Africa.

And the group emphasizes education that reaches far beyond the one-week festival—and the confines of Provincetown. An emphasis on Williams and his work as the hub of a wheel—with other like-minded playwrights' work circling around it—has changed the way teachers and drama historians are positioning Williams's work, says Kaplan, himself a Williams scholar.

In a July 27, 2009 article in the British newspaper the *Guardian*, noted drama critic Michael Billington comments on the evolution of the global view of Williams's work.

> *Thankfully, we have gotten over the idea that Williams is a sexual sensationalist. Now, we tend to emphasize his lyric, compassionate side. He has been described as "the poet of lost souls," and we tend to dwell on his empathy with the spiritually wounded. In this reading, the keynote line is that of the itinerant Val in Williams' * Orpheus Descending *who says: "We're all of us sentenced to solitary confinement inside our own skins, for life!"*
>
> *I'd be the last to deny Williams's poignant poetry and echoing loneliness, but we overlook the more robust side of his talent. His plays offer a devastating portrait of the ugly prejudices of the American south; they acknowledge economic realities; and, in the spirit of his admired Chekhov, are as comic as they are tragic.*

While Williams was not without recognition in his own time—he was awarded two Pulitzers and the Presidential Medal of Freedom—the scope and breadth of his work are now being recognized, thanks in part to the scholars associated with the Tennessee Williams Festival. This master, who, like Eugene O'Neill, penned some of his greatest works amid the dunes and sea shanties of Provincetown, is now viewed in the company of some of history's greatest dramatists.

Closeup: David Drake, Artistic Director, Provincetown Theater/New Provincetown Players

According to David Drake, there is an "invisible bloodline that runs from Cape Cod theater's earliest beginnings in Provincetown, throughout this spit of land that juts out into the sea." With the birth of American drama at the tip of Cape Cod, he says, an energy developed and spread across the region.

"A lot of people who were in the theater community in Provincetown got involved in other theaters. For instance, the founder of the Cape Playhouse [Raymond Moore] was one of the Provincetown Players. And you see this replayed in theaters up and down the Cape," he says.

Drake says that energy is almost palpable, especially in the summer, when audiences sample theatrical fare around them, almost like diners enjoying a smorgasbord.

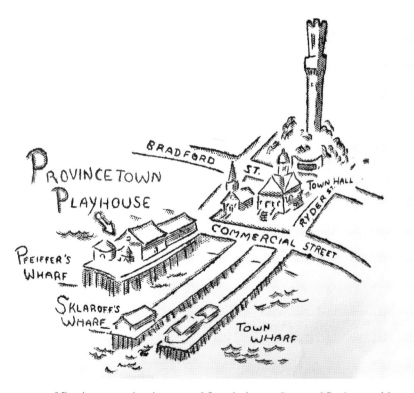

Vintage map of Provincetown, showing map of first playhouse. *Courtesy of Provincetown Museum.*

"There are so many options around that the level of performance just naturally rises. People who come to the Cape for theater are sophisticated and discerning; they want a variety of experiences, and want them to be distinct. They might go to WHAT [the Wellfleet Harbor Actors Theatre] for one production, then over to the Academy [Academy of Performing Arts], then come here. And they expect it all to be top quality—like a dinner that's rich and satisfying, but also nourishing."

Moving Outward from the Birthplace of American Drama

So the unique art form that we now recognize as American theater—with its emphasis on realism and experimentation—took root in Provincetown (and, of course, New York) and began spreading outward. On Cape Cod, that has meant the establishment of theater troupes (both professional and amateur) in virtually every town along the peninsula. Some groups (like the Woods Hole Actors Theatre) perform in available community spaces, while others have longtime homes in historic buildings (the Academy of Performing Arts in Orleans and the Barnstable Comedy Club included). Still others (including the Wellfleet Harbor Actors Theatre and Cape Cod Community College's Tilden Arts Center) have constructed state-of-the-art facilities to house their productions and educational activities.

In the succeeding chapters, I'll be your guide for a tour of Cape Cod that moves outward from Provincetown and looks at the histories and current roles of theater groups we encounter along the way, along with a nod to groups that were a part of the fabric of Cape Cod theater in the past. By the end of the tour, I hope it will be crystal clear that Cape Cod theater is the descendant of a movement that began more than one hundred years ago with a little one-act play called *Bound East for Cardiff* on a wharf in Provincetown.

3

THEATER HISTORY
ON THE LOWER CAPE

DRAMA AND MUSIC IN THE DUNES

Moving out of Provincetown, with its wharves jutting out into the harbor, houses nestled together and hugging narrow streets and constant bustle (at least for three or four months a year), the land, sea and sky seem to expand into infinity. The dunes rise like giant sandcastles around you, and sky and sea seem to meld together and go on forever. On windy days, gulls fly over curling whitecaps and the Atlantic leaps and dives, nearly covering the dunes.

PAYOMET PERFORMING ARTS CENTER

The first stop on our trek up-Cape is Truro. High on a hill in North Truro is the Payomet Performing Arts Center, its name a reminder of the original residents of the area, the Wampanoag Native Americans, who called the area Pamet or Payomet. The center was established in 1998 by professional stage and film actor Guy Strauss, who gratefully called Truro home. In keeping with its lofty locale, the center has had lofty goals from the very beginning. Strauss was determined to bring to the lower Cape productions featuring trained professional actors and directors. Over the years, actors, directors and technical professionals have come from major markets, including Boston, New York and the West Coast.

In the beginning, the company—which at that point had limited audience capacity—focused on theatrical productions, often debuting new works and

Sand dunes on the Lower Cape. *GoodPhotos*.

offering a home to new playwrights. Now "the tent on the hill," with its seating capacity at 1,000, also hosts concerts featuring noted performers like Judy Collins, Laura Nyro, Tom Rush and Taj Mahal, as well as up-and-coming artists. Current managing artistic director Kevin Rice says the center's attention to musical programming and expansive capacity puts it "in the same league as the Melody Tent," the Cape's noted summer musical venue. (Located in Hyannis, the "Tent" seats 1,500. As we venture farther up-Cape, we will of course include a history of the site, a summer tradition for more than sixty years.)

And, making ultimate use of the impressive capacity under the big top, the center now also presents an annual Cirque du Soleil–style circus. (Fittingly—considering the center's seaside locale—the 2018 circus offering was entitled *The Scurvy Urchin*.)

Here is how Rice defines the work of his center:

> *Our diverse programming can be summed up as outside-the-box and inside-the-community. Our audiences have come to expect national talent on the local stage whether in the form of Grammy-winning music artists and*

emerging young stars, or at our summer theater productions showcasing professional actors and directors from around the country. We produce more shows all the time at various venues, especially in the off-season, including at the First Congregational Church in Wellfleet, at Wellfleet Preservation Hall, and at Provincetown Town Hall.

Like the center's originator, Rice is an award-winning playwright, director and actor. His plays have been produced at the Edinburgh Fringe, in Russia and in New York. And, in keeping with the center's commitment to "incubating new works," Payomet recently featured Rice's original work *Hopper's Ghost*, a production in the tradition of *Spoon River Anthology*. Several of his plays have also been produced by the Wellfleet Harbor Actors Theater, including *Oblomov*, which was greeted with rave reviews.

Here's what the article "Snore of the Crowd a Sign of the Success of Oblomov," in the September 3, 2012 edition of the *Boston Globe*, had to say about the production:

> *A theater where you're actively encouraged to fall asleep? Or, failing that, to participate in a snoring chorus? Welcome to Oblomovka, ancestral home of Russian napper extraordinaire Ilya Ilyich Oblomov, the fictional subject of Ivan Goncharov's 1859 novel and now Kevin Rice's delightfully capricious dramatization at the Wellfleet Harbor Actors Theater.*
>
> *As the play opens, we find Oblomov (Michael Pemberton) in a dream state—his favored habitat. His father (Michael Samuel Kaplan) enlists our aid in protecting and prolonging this hallowed idyll, as his bossy, cosseting mother (Valerie Stanford) waits on her fully adult—and then some—baby hand and foot, proffering sweetmeats in his rare moments of wakefulness. Pies and blintzes are on the menu; at one point she invites the audience to partake of warm rolls—"from the Stop & Shop!"*

Like so many theaters on the peninsula, Payomet also dedicates time and energy to education, with a unique offering for area young people. Along with theater arts classes, the center offers a circus arts camp during the summer months.

Summing up his theater's approach, Rice says: "Above all the tent is alive and eclectic. You can feel it during the spellbound moments of a fully-staged professional theater production, or under the colored lights and open night sky of our outdoor dance floor. And then there are moments on a sunny summer morning as parents sit on picnic benches waiting for a children's theater class to end. The tent is alive. It's all magical."

And that, fellow travelers, is a pretty good description of theater on Cape Cod.

Wellfleet Harbor Actors Theatre: A Legendary Beginning

You could almost say that the Wellfleet Harbor Actors Theatre (WHAT) in Wellfleet had its genesis in a very well-timed cup of coffee. It was 1985, and six theater artists who had been informally bound together in a group they called the Outer Cape Performance Group were chatting over cups of coffee at Uncle Frank's, a then-popular coffee shop on the harbor. They had been working together for a few years, mounting modest productions in church basements, restaurants, friends' homes and other found spaces. That day, they heard that a space was open in the same building as Uncle Frank's, and that signaled the group's reincarnation as WHAT.

The very first production by the newly named group was the avant-garde playwright Eugène Ionesco's first full-length play, *Rhinoceros*. The show, which is a thinly veiled treatise on the dangers of totalitarianism, spins the tale of a French town dealing with the unlikely visit of a rhinoceros on its main street. The show established the group's reputation as a somewhat quirky, experimental troupe grounded in a community dedicated to unique artistic expression. (That dedication is evident in the cluster of galleries, shops and cafés that line the streets around the town's downtown harbor.)

Even in that early period, one of the theater's biggest fans and supporters was Julie Harris, often deemed the First Lady of American Theater. (Her portrayal of Emily Dickinson in *The Belle of Amherst* on Broadway in 1976 won her a Tony and a place in theater history.) The actress said this about her early experience with WHAT, as quoted in an August 26, 2013 article, "With Love to Julie Harris," on the CapeCodToday website. (The article was published shortly after her death.): "I've been going to WHAT since I first moved to Chatham. My first production was *American Buffalo* in 1985, a thrilling experience, and I have had many, many more every season at WHAT. Great theater has the power to transform the way we see, the way we feel, and WHAT performs wonderfully stimulating, challenging theater."

In 1991, Harris performed for WHAT for the first time, opposite George Grizzard, in a one-night performance of *Love Letters*. Over the next few years, the company steadily grew in size and stature, soon attracting audiences from all over New England and performers from the Boston and New York markets. During that period, noted actor and director Jeff Zinn (son of socialist historian Howard Zinn) came on the scene as artistic director, and the company began to grow "exponentially," according to current managing director and artistic associate Christopher Ostrom. (Ostrom first came to WHAT in 1997 as a lighting designer and has since designed more than fifty productions for the company. In 2013, he took on his current role.)

Julie Harris. Washington Post.

By the first years of the new century, the theater was regularly selling out its ninety-seat harbor-side theater. And its popularity got an additional shot in the arm when Harris agreed to be honorary chair of the theater's board of directors and, subsequently, to star in Martin McDonagh's *The Beauty Queen of Leenane*. The show was so popular that the company added extra performances to accommodate long lines of fans.

It had become clear that the troupe needed room to grow. So, in 2006, the company broke ground on its 250-seat, state-of-the-art facility aside Cape Cod's Route 6, fittingly dubbing its new stage after its famous supporter.

"Julie didn't want the theater named after her, but she was fine with us giving the stage her name," Ostrom says. Theater archives show Harris in a hard hat at the ground-breaking ceremony of the new facility. For years, Harris attended every show in the theater, until her eventual ill health.

Former artistic director Dan Lombardo wrote this about the opening night of the new stage for the August 23, 2013 edition of the online publication CapeCodToday.

On June 23, 2007, with a standing-room-only audience, I had the honor of escorting Ms. Harris into the theater. We sat her in the center of the front row. Having suffered a stroke in 2001, we asked if, after the speeches, she would simply stand to accept the cheers that would undoubtedly follow.

When the time came, WHAT staff members brought two dozen red roses to her seat. She stood—then leapt onto the stage. Her face beaming, she kissed the palm of her hand, knelt down and slapped the deck of the Julie Harris Stage. A stage was born.

From that moment, the all-pro theater has been dedicated, says Ostrom, to "summer theater that isn't summer theater. We're somewhere between Provincetown and The Cape Playhouse—both geographically and spiritually." He continues: "Actually, we like to see ourselves as descendants of the original Provincetown Players because of the new works we've always supported. I'm convinced there are more theaters here than in some areas of Manhattan. People want more meat on their plates. Our audiences are incredibly intelligent, thoughtful and demanding. We've developed a reputation for doing edgy, audacious fare."

For example, back in 2001, WHAT presented what *Playbill* called in a July 27, 2001 article "the raunchy *Cooking with Elvis*, a black comedy about a baker named Stuart who finds himself sucked into the lives of an extremely dysfunctional family. They are a paraplegic Elvis impersonator, his alcoholic, sex-crazed wife, his food-obsessed daughter and their pet tortoise named Stanley." Oscar-nominated author Lee Hall is best known for scripting the hit (and very different) film *Billy Elliot*.

Seventeen years later, the troupe dished up another food-related production, *Raging Skillet*, a comedy about Chef Rossi, who developed a whole career—and new art form—out of her determination to show her mother it was possible to cook without a microwave. In the process, she became New York's number one (and maybe only) punk rock chef and learned to appreciate her parents. During the show, the actress playing Rossi actually cooked onstage.

These days, the company treats the facility as a campus, often using the Julie Harris Stage for its major productions while erecting a tent on the grounds for other works, including children's programming. But even children's programming has a bit of an edge. For instance, a 2018 production of *The Magic Cloak* included some sharply satirical lines about President Donald Trump.

"I think audacious is a really good word for us. After all, it was pretty audacious of six artists in a coffee shop to start a theater company," Ostrom says. "At WHAT we believe theater is absolutely central to modern culture. Really, it's the modern equivalent of storytelling around a campfire, and we believe it's critical that it survives."

Right: WHAT, *A Midsummer Night's Dream*, 2016. *Michael and Suz Karchmer*.

Below: WHAT, *The Raging Skillet*, 2018. *Michael and Suz Karchmer*.

When WHAT made its "audacious" move to the state-of-the-art campus near Route 6, it vacated its onetime home on the Wellfleet Harbor.

That provided the perfect opportunity for another group to take up residence.

The Iconic Seaside Theater on the Harbor: The Harbor Stage Company

In 2012, a group of professionals with ties to Wellfleet and the region joined forces to bring a completely artist-run ensemble to what the group calls the "iconic seaside theater." In fact, the group stands as one of the only completely artist-run companies in the country. The principals claim that, "Our artists are as likely to be found in a rehearsal as they are selling tickets at the box office or planning our latest fundraiser. We sweep, we poster, we balance the books—the result is a comprehensively informed ensemble that measures success in terms of artistic ideals instead of the bottom line."

Predictably, the group of experienced theater artists produces plays that are sometimes as iconic as their theater and sometimes entirely new and cutting edge. Since the group's inaugural year, it has produced more than twenty plays, among them Henrik Ibsen's *Hedda Gabler* and *A Doll's House*, Anton Chekhov's *The Seagull*, an adaptation of Ingmar Bergman's *Persona* by ensemble member Robert Kropf (a world premiere) and *Who's Afraid of Virginia Woolf?* by Edward Albee.

Kropf, the company's artistic director, worked with WHAT under then–artistic director Jeff Zinn and has worked with both American Repertory Theatre and Boston Center for the Arts. Other ensemble members include Jonathan Fielding, originally from Texas, who has been part of the Broadway productions of *Pygmalion*, *The Seagull* and *Noises Off*; Stacy Fischer, an actor and educator in the Boston area who works with Deana's Educational Theater and Theatre Espresso on developing and performing comprehensive educational theater programs; and Brenda Withers, an actor and playwright who has appeared in productions around the country. Her original works include *Matt & Ben*, *The Ding Dongs* and *String Around My Finger*, which was awarded Portland Stage's Clauder Prize.

Clearly, the Harbor Stage is becoming a center on Cape Cod for serious and thought-provoking theater. But the group also prides itself on keeping good theater affordable, putting it within reach of a wide range of theater lovers.

Speaking of "thought-provoking" theater, one group in the history of theater in Wellfleet stands out, the now—unfortunately—disbanded Fisherman's Players.

THE FISHERMAN'S PLAYERS: FISHING FOR SOULS AND MINDS

The history of theater on Cape Cod is filled with one fascinating gem after another. But every now and then, when researching the vast landscape of a subject like this, you come across a bit of history that stands out. That's the case with the Fisherman's Players, a group organized in 1964 by the Reverend Richard D. Waters and once based in the Wellfleet Methodist Church and later in the town of Eastham. It was an age of social revolution in the country, and Waters was dedicated to dealing with the issues of the day not only from the pulpit, but also onstage.

Waters was born in Virginia and educated in drama and art at a number of D.C.-area colleges, eventually also earning his divinity degree at Boston University. He went from Virginia to Hollywood, where he produced and directed a number of works for radio, TV and the silver screen, directing three films for 20th Century Fox and mounting a number of plays for the area's Metro Playhouse, including *Key Largo* and Eugene O'Neill's *Suds in Your Eye*. Back on the East Coast, he produced two plays for the Off-Broadway stage, *Glass Menagerie* and *Angel Street*, a play about a family in nineteenth-century London by Patrick Hamilton. And he did a three-year stint with the Globe Repertory Theatre Company in D.C.

Eventually, Waters made his way a little farther north, where he established the Trinity Square Playhouse in Providence. He inevitably found his way to Cape Cod, where he first did some acting with the Falmouth Playhouse (whose history we'll explore later in the book), finally establishing the Fisherman's Players at his church in Wellfleet. In her *Theater on Cape Cod*, Evelyn Lawson includes the following quote from Waters describing the beginnings of his troupe.

> *It was a startling thing for a new minister to ask the members of his church to go along with him on a project so foreign to church procedures. To attempt the program, the church had to create the facilities for making theatrical production possible. It is to their credit that the church members were far-sighted enough to see the advantages of such a program, especially when you add the fact that the dramas were not going to be used to win new members*

or make money for the church. And that the real motive for the program was to communicate the higher human values to the world at-large, and that those who participated would be drawn from all races, all faiths and all walks of life.

And that, in a clamshell, defines Waters's goals for his players. Or, as Lawson notes in her book: "[He] has administered social shock treatments couched within the matrix of the Players' productions. He makes no apologies for portraying messages. But in delivering these messages he has not sacrificed his high artistic production standards or lost his appreciation of theater as an art form."

In the end, Waters wrote, produced and in many cases played in between thirty and forty plays with religious themes. (Some that have been referred to in one publication or another have unfortunately been lost.) And he created another sizable body of work focusing on contemporary themes like overpopulation, destruction of the environment, race relations and equality for women. Works, some of which were produced while he served as manager of a playhouse in MacLean, Virginia, and some while he worked with the Players in Wellfleet and later Eastham, include *Andersonville*; *Jesus, Son of Man*; *Shadow and Substance*; *Crown of Thorns*; *Fistful of Earth*; *Long Road to the Mountain*; and *Black Messiah*. Some of his works were one-acts, some—like *A Modern Faust*—were adaptations, and his body of work includes a number of full-length original works. He also collaborated with the likes of Norman Mailer and Judge Francis Biddle on Biddle's play *The Trial of William Penn*. Judge Biddle, a former attorney general of the United States, also served as the primary judge at the postwar Nuremberg trials.

The Players were at the time Cape Cod's only repertory theater, meaning they mounted plays from a specific list of works—in this case, from Waters's repertoire. The group's resident company was complemented by professional theater techs and stage managers, resulting in critically acclaimed productions. For example, when longtime *Boston Globe* drama critic Kevin Kelly reviewed the group's first production in Wellfleet, *Truant Apostle*, he gushed: "Dick Waters is totally unfair. He has written and produced a play that makes us think. That's a shock to the average playgoer's system."

In her book, Lawson describes the reaction, expressed during a postproduction roundtable discussion, of one obviously conservative playgoer to the group's production of the play *The Green Man*:

A woman who had seen the play said, "Such language, such terrible language, and in a church too! Last week I saw a show at the Cape Playhouse and there was swearing all through it. Then I went to the Falmouth Playhouse in the hope it would be a nice play, but it was worse. Then I thought the Fisherman's Players, under the auspices of the church, was bound to be less profane. But tonight there were more swear words than I have ever heard on any stage."

Reverend Waters replied, "When the man on the street stops swearing, I promise there will not be one swear word in any of my plays."

The popularity of the group meant that it soon outgrew the Wellfleet church's stage and an additional stage at the Eastham Wellfleet Church. According to information supplied by Waters's son West Waters:

Supporting members of the community and powers within the Southern New England Conference of the United Methodist Church came together, and a property on Route 6 in Eastham was made available. A steel building was erected and a 225-seat venue was built to house a theater. Waters then continued the theater work full-time, sponsored by the United Methodist Board of Missions as an outreach program dedicated to the current issues of the day. In front of the theater building was a 200-year-old former inn and stagecoach stop with 13 small rooms. There, the family resided and many of the actors were housed for each summer season, and the Players mounted as many as four shows a week in the summer season.

As well as mounting plays in Wellfleet, the group went on the road with some productions, eventually traveling to twenty-two states. One play the group took on the road was *The Black Messiah*, a work about the race war in the United States, with Malcolm X at its center. In 1968, three years after the assassination of the firebrand, Waters and his Players took the play on a road trip around the Northeast. After a one-night booking in New York City, he was interviewed on the local NPR station on September 16 of that year. It's an amazing recording, in which the ever-articulate Waters describes the play and his work with the Players and how it all fit in with the engine of change driving society at the time. At one point, he says:

We're concerned with communicating human need; we're concerned with the interpretation of human value with regard to social issues. I don't

*think there's any such thing as "art for art's sake." I think that whenever
an artist records something or goes through the painful process of putting
it down, one man creates that another man might experience. And so our
main concern is that of communication—the communication of value,
or perhaps the encountering of the confusing issues of our times to try to
determine what is value, so we have something to say in every play we do.*

In an August 28, 1990 article published at the time of Waters's death in a
Virginia newspaper, the *Daily Press*, one of his players described his influence
on actors as well as on theatergoers. He and his wife, Maria, had disbanded
the Wellfleet group in 1979 and returned to Virginia, where Waters became
pastor of a church on Virginia's Eastern Shore. The couple then moved to
Isle of Wight County in 1985, where Richard became pastor at two local
churches. At that point, he reestablished the Players and took productions
all over the state.

According to the *Daily Press* article, with his professional dedication to
excellence, he often had to put shows together on a shoestring budget. Still,
he was able to inspire the people he worked with. The article notes that one
of his regular actors, Becky Gwaltney, said, "he gave her the confidence to
speak in front of large groups of people, and eventually serve as lay minister
in the United Methodist Church." She added, "I think he saw himself as a
fisher of men, a fisher of souls. And it wasn't all from the pulpit."

In the same article, Maria Waters describes her surprising—and
ultimately enormously satisfying—life with "a fisher of souls." "'I thought I
had married a man who would become a very wealthy theater director and
take me to New York,' she said. His new career sparked her own 'journey of
faith,' and eventually she, too, became a minister."

In the article, Maria goes on to say that her husband considered his plays
to be "prophetic sermons" on the state of modern society, but that he balked
at publishing them. "The creative instinct in him could never accept a play
as finished," she said.

Maria explains in the article that, along with his "24-hour consuming
passion with theater," he was almost as passionate about fishing. Several
times a week, he took his boat out on Cypress Creek in Rescue, Virginia.
One day in late August 1990, he never made it home after his fishing trip.
He had succumbed to an apparent heart attack and had fallen overboard.
He was sixty-three years old.

According to the article, a number of friends and family members used
the word *genius* "to describe a playwright whose stern and confrontational

religious drama seemed at odds with an easygoing charm that encouraged people to confide in him."

Richard Waters died on the water he loved, fishing. This is once again proof that truth is stranger—and more dramatic—than fiction. No playwright could have written a more fitting conclusion to the life of this "fisher of souls."

Orleans Arena Theatre and Academy of Performing Arts

Just two towns up-Cape from Wellfleet is the town of Orleans. With its bustling harbor and busy town center, it is a center of activity on the Lower Cape. On a hill near the center of town stands a venerable building, the Academy Playhouse/Orleans Arena Theatre. One of the Cape's historic theaters, the building actually began life in 1873 as the Orleans town hall.

Then, in the late 1940s, the legendary originators of the Orleans Arena Theatre, Gordon and Betsy Argo, arrived in town. By that time, the town was ready to move its offices out of the house on the hill, providing the perfect opportunity for the inveterate theater people to use the space and put down roots. The couple established the theater in 1950, which meant that the building on the hill has been used continually as a theater for almost seventy years. And here's the important thing about the theater's name: It was the first summer residence arena theater (theater-in-the-round) in the United States. (If you think about it, an arena theater is the perfect way to bring an audience directly into the action onstage. It's especially effective for staging intimate scenes between just a few characters, making the audience feel a part of the scene. And it of course has its roots in early Greek and medieval staging.)

From 1950 through 1976, the Arena was a theater-in-residence. Students from George Washington University worked and performed at the theater and lived in a house just up the hill. The theater was home to young actors, actresses and technicians who quite literally grew up together as they developed their craft, meanwhile staging a new production every week. The group offered shows ranging from dramas like William Inge's *Dark at the Top of the Stairs* to comedies like *Bell, Book and Candle* to ensemble pieces like *Dames at Sea*. At its peak, the theater had thirty-five artists-in-residence living and working together as a theater colony.

Above: Arena Theatre,
circa 1954. *Quinn
Photography*.

Right: Arena Theatre, *Bell,
Book and Candle*, 1958.
Quinn Photography.

54

In fact, theaters-in-residence have been a time-honored tradition on Cape Cod. While the Academy, the successor of the Arena, now only works with a few interns a year, the Monomoy Theatre in Chatham and the College Light Opera Company in Falmouth—both of which will be spotlighted later—have had active dramatic-arts-in-residence programs for their summer seasons.

In *Stagestruck: Confessions from Summer Stock*, a docudrama about life and work at the Arena produced by film producer Liz Argo, Gordon and Betsy's daughter, alum Kurt Vonnegut talks about his time at the theater. "People really would work *this* hard for nothing. And they would, because that's theater!" In an American Public Television clip featuring his quote, there are scenes of actors sewing costumes, carrying lumber and practicing sword fights.

Vonnegut, who would go on to win both a Hugo and a Drama Desk award, wrote *Penelope* at the theater, where it was first produced. The work was later produced as the film *Happy Birthday, Wanda June*—which won the writer his Drama Desk. According to Liz, Vonnegut—who was a longtime summer resident of the Cape—remained a faithful supporter of the theater and Argo family throughout his life. (He was also actively involved with another theater, the Barnstable Comedy Club. But that's a story for another chapter.)

Shortly after Betsy's death in 2016, in a March 6 article in the *Cape Cod Times*, the Argo's other daughter, Allison, said this about her mother's love of theater and its impact on her own life. "I really remember so clearly being a little girl and sitting in the balcony every night, and watching my mother play one of the Tennessee Williams characters on stage, and I would just sit up there and cry," she said. "I think what is really seared in my memory and in my heart is how much soul and how much history was there unfolding on the stage and behind the scenes."

In that same 2016 article in the *Cape Cod Times*, professional actor and former Argo student Ron Jacoby, who spent the summer of 1953 at the theater, said this about Betsy: "She was theater from head to toe. She was sort of mother to the company. That first season was incredible. I absolutely fell in love with the theater."

Young actors like Jacoby often performed alongside the Argo siblings, Allison, Liz and brother Walter. In fact, according to Liz, their mother often chose plays that would offer roles for her offspring. One good example is *Dark at the Top of the Stairs*, in which Betsy and Liz (fittingly enough) played mother and daughter.

"I was just 3 years old when I first stepped foot on stage," Liz says. And she was no stranger to the stage at the nearby Harwich Junior Theatre (now the Cape Cod Theatre Company), where, she says, "I learned to cry

Arena Theatre, Betsy and Liz Argo in
Dark at the Top of the Stairs, 1963. *Quinn
Photography*.

on-command." And by the time she was a teenager, she was managing productions. "I'll never forget the day Mom fired the stage manager and got me out of bed to take on the job. I was 14 or 15," she says.

In fact, the Argo children were an integral part of the theater-colony-on-the hill in Orleans. Liz says the company was like one big family. "I feel like we had a whole company of parents; we were really raised by the residents." She remembers washing dinner dishes "for two hours. There were no dishwashers back then." And she talks about driving her mother around town to hang show posters. "It was the only chance I got to leave the grounds. Otherwise we were just at the theater."

Both Allison and Liz went on to careers in show business, with Allison initially pursuing an acting career, including roles in two Broadway productions and roles in two made-for-TV movies and a TV series. She has also been an award-winning film producer, director, writer, editor and narrator best known for documentaries that focus on endangered wildlife and conservation. Liz became a script supervisor and has also managed a film production company of her own.

The senior Argos were divorced in the 1960s, and Betsy ran the Arena for more than a decade on her own. Finally, by the middle of the next decade, she was ready to move on. Luckily for theatergoers on the Lower Cape, that was not the end of the historic theater's story.

THE ARENA BECOMES THE ACADEMY

In 1975, another noted theater couple, John and Elizabeth Kelly, began using the theater for their Academy of Performing Arts. They began offering classes in music, dance and drama to the community, providing the impetus for a group of local theater-lovers to form a board of directors and incorporate under the new name, also purchasing the playhouse as the group's permanent home.

From those early days on, the group has been dedicated to community theater, using amateur actors in its 162-seat theater. In fact, according to previous artistic director Peter Earle, the group's charter states that it will use unpaid actors. He notes that, these days, a commitment to community theater can sometimes make it difficult to compete in a competitive theater environment like Cape Cod's, saying, "More and more theater companies are beginning to use paid actors."

But operating as a community theater has never kept the Academy from mounting ambitious productions, including such classics as *Les Miserables*, *Grease*, *La Cage aux Folles* and *Driving Miss Daisy*. And the company is no stranger to drama and experimental theater, with shows like *Amadeus*, *A*

Academy of Performing Arts, *Fiddler on the Roof*, 2003. *Quinn Photography*.

Gentleman's Guide to Love and Murder, *Fiddler on the Roof* and *Cabaret* among the more than 450 (at this writing) productions the Academy has mounted. (*A Gentleman's Guide* was a regional premiere.)

Obviously, the sheer volume of the productions at the Playhouse has made it a fertile breeding ground for theater talent on Cape Cod. Over the years, actors and technicians have moved outward from their incubator at the Academy to theater groups dotting the Cape, including the Chatham Drama Guild, Cape Cod Repertory Theatre in Brewster and the Cape Playhouse in Dennis. In this way, Earle says, the Playhouse has been a major contributor to the thriving theater culture on Cape Cod.

"There are more than thirty theater companies dotting Cape Cod, and still we draw audiences from as far away as Sandwich and Provincetown [two ends of Cape Cod]. And it's not unusual to have audience members from as far away as Saskatchewan. The Cape is an amazing theater environment, with people actually moving here because of the theater life," Earle says.

At the end of this century's second decade, the Academy suffered through that often-fatal theater disease: lack of funds. By the end of 2018, the organization was almost literally buried in debt, with a deficit of $400,000. Trying to operate both the Playhouse and School proved an almost

Academy of Performing Arts, *Cabaret*, 2018. *Michael and Suz Karchmer.*

impossible task. That strain prompted a four-month hiatus, with the road ahead unclear at that point. But, thanks to the concerted efforts of a number of community members and longtime Playhouse supporters, the group was able to begin to regain its footing in 2019 with productions of *Frozen* and *Sleepy Hollow* and a haunted house that brought in more than five hundred ghosts and goblins. And, as of this printing, the Academy is planning a full summer schedule of productions—all Cape premieres—for 2020. Efforts are now underway to reduce financial strain by bringing school programs into the Playhouse, eventually making the classic building an arts complex/community resource.

In a February 8, 2020 *Cape Cod Times* article, entertainment editor/arts writer Kathi Scrizzi Driscoll quotes new Academy president Judy Hamer as she voiced the sentiments of the Lower Cape theater community. Hamer, longtime drama director at the area's Nauset Regional High School, said, "I love this building. I want to save it."

Elements Theatre Company

Another Orleans-based group is the Elements Theatre Company, a group of sixteen artists-in-residence affiliated with a Christian religious sect called The Church of the Transfiguration. Like the Harbor Stage in Wellfleet, the company is committed to serious, often classical theater. In keeping with its religious bent, the group's website (www.elementstheatre.org) states: "Dedicated to exploring the deepest truths of the human condition through dramatic storytelling and imaginative stagecraft, we perform both classical and classically-rooted modern works year-round."

The group's productions have included Ralph Vaughan Williams's operatic interpretation of John Bunyan's *The Pilgrim's Progress*, Shakespeare's *King Lear* and *A Merchant of Venice*, a dramatic telling of Dickens's *A Christmas Carol* and Noël Coward's *Blithe Spirit*.

As we move on to the "elbow" of Cape Cod, we'll explore a quartet of theater companies that can boast long and distinguished histories, making them integral parts of the fabric of the Cape's theater world.

4

THEATER AT THE ELBOW OF THE CAPE

DEDICATION AND DETERMINATION

Chatham and Harwich, two picturesque towns nestled in the elbow of Cape Cod, are home to three of the oldest theaters on Cape Cod. Monomoy Theatre and the Chatham Drama Guild in Chatham and the Cape Cod Theatre Company/Home of the Harwich Junior Theatre, can each boast decades of service to the summer theater-loving community. And, like so many theaters on Cape Cod, both Monomoy and the Cape Cod Theatre Company have been dedicated to teaching the theater craft, as well as mounting several productions a year. (Note: As of this printing, the future of Monomoy is unclear, but the theater still stands as a symbol of the Cape's rich theater history. More on this shortly.)

The Cape Cod Repertory Theatre in Brewster, on the other hand, is a newer addition to the local theater scene and is a company of professional actors dedicated to often groundbreaking original and experimental pieces.

MONOMOY THEATRE: A HERITAGE OF WINDMILLS AND WHIRLIGIGS

The buildings that now house Monomoy (which comes from Chatham's original name, Constablewick Momomoit) and formerly its summer company once constituted the homestead of Chatham resident Washington Taylor. Following an extension of Chatham's Main Street in the mid-nineteenth century, the businessman saw the potential of the virgin territory and so

Monomoy Theatre, *A Little Night Music*, 2017. *Michael and Suz Karchmer.*

moved his general store and homestead to a group of buildings on the new extension. There he reestablished his general store and also operated a livery and blacksmith shop.

By the end of the century, the town was fast becoming a summer tourist destination (thanks in part to the railroad that by that time was running up and down the Cape). With the end of World War I, the tourist trade in town grew exponentially, and tourist-related businesses began to spring up on the town's Main Street. (Some things never change; Chatham's Main Street is a popular tourist destination to this day.)

One of the new businesses was a toy factory, which occupied the former Taylor homestead and produced working windmills and whirligigs for tourists trying to keep youngsters occupied. (Again, some things never change.) It seems somehow fitting that a theater—itself dedicated to fantasy and flights of fancy—should take up residence in a building that was once a toy factory/store. By this time, previous owner Washington Taylor had sold the property to toy manufacturer Stella A. Gill. But, as Robert Davis notes in his book *A History of Monomoy Theatre*, local legend has it that "Washy's" spirit still resides in the rafters of the old playhouse. (Interestingly, Washy is not the only phantom who shows up in Cape Cod theater lore. More on that later.)

Gill eventually sold the factory to Chatham resident Judge Charles Bassett, who himself soon tired of trying to keep the factory's whirligigs spinning. In 1934, he sold the factory to local artist Harold Dunbar, who dreamed of renovating the old barn/toy factory into a working theater and thus creating an arts center in Chatham. Dunbar—who local legend has it was something of an eccentric, with a bright yellow car, a schooner named *Ivory Soap* (it floats) and his own arts column in a local paper—had been fully immersed in the arts renaissance that was sweeping across the Cape.

As we discussed in earlier chapters, the arts revolution began in Provincetown with visual artists, writers, dramatists and actors flocking to the art colony at the tip of the Cape in numbers that rivaled the seagulls that flocked to Cape Cod shores. Clearly, it was inevitable that artists of every stripe would venture outward and impact the culture along the peninsula. (As we noted earlier, Raymond Moore, founder of the Cape Playhouse, was originally with the Provincetown Players.) And a perfect storm was brewing (in a good way) that was creating fertile ground for the growth of theater arts on the Cape generally and in Chatham specifically.

First, as we said earlier, the tourist trade had been growing in leaps and bounds since the final decades of the nineteenth century. That created a ready audience for Broadway producers whose summer audiences were limited to the few hearty souls willing to sit in a stifling theater in Manhattan's dog days. They found those audiences at venues like the Cape Playhouse in Dennis and the Melody Tent in Hyannis. (Both venues still offer entertainment, with the nearly century-old Playhouse still mounting shows featuring professional artists based on both coasts and the Melody Tent now bringing in popular musical talent.)

In some places along the Cape, homegrown, community theaters were taking root. For instance, in the mid-Cape area, the almost-century-old Barnstable Comedy Club stands as a monument to those early days. (See the next chapter.) In Chatham, thanks to a group of locals—including, of course, the ubiquitous Harold Dunbar—the Chatham Drama Guild formed in 1931 with no permanent home of its own. (It was to gain a state charter in 1937.) For a few years, the company performed in local churches and other found spaces, as is often the fate of newly formed community theaters. So, when Dunbar purchased the old toy factory, he had a theater company ready to take to the boards. Actually, the Guild performed in the theater in the off-season for forty years before renovating its space on Crowell Road in Chatham to include its own (heated) theater. During those years, the property was known as the Guildhouse.

Then, in 1938, Dunbar sold the theater to Mary Winslow, a local heiress who had caught the bug for the theater arts at Smith College. After graduation, she was determined to come back home and establish a professional company in Chatham. So—following an ambitious renovation project—she began bringing companies of professional actors and directors to the theater for the summer season. It was Winslow who dubbed the theater Monomoy in honor of the town's early name, and the name has stuck to this day.

What followed was a golden age of theater, not only at Monomoy but also across Cape Cod. In his history of Monomoy, Davis notes:

> *To be there in the theater on Cape Cod in the 1930s, 40s and 50s was to share some impressive company. Consider the following cast list: Gertrude Lawrence, Henry Fonda, Helen Hayes, Humphrey Bogart, Ethel Barrymore, Robert Montgomery, Uta Hagen, Walter Matthau, Eva Le Gallienne, Bette Davis, Edward Everett Horton, Ruth Gordon, Tallulah Bankhead, Dana Andrews, Beatrice Lillie, John Garfield, Jessica Tandy, Hume Cronyn, Lillian Gish and Paulette Goddard. And that only begins to tell the tale of Cape Cod's golden age of summer theater.*

Winslow is revered in Chatham and across the Cape Cod theater world— justifiably so—for her part in forging that golden age. Not only did she consistently plan renovations on the old, historic building—preserving it as part of Cape Cod theater history—but every season, she also brought to the Cape actors, directors and technicians with impeccable credentials, many of whom came back season after season. Period photos show actors and technicians in little groups around the grounds, presumably discussing productions. Every season, those productions ran the gamut from light comedy to new experimental works to melodrama, usually with a cozy little murder mystery thrown in for good measure. And, as Davis points out, "the season often concluded with the elegant wit of Noel Coward."

After the 1942 season, the theater's doors were closed in recognition of World War II. When the war ended, Winslow came back from a stint with the Women's Army Corps to get the neglected theater back in shape. The doors reopened in 1948 and continued under Winslow's auspices almost until her death in 1957. With no one to take the helm, the theater once again went up for sale.

But another strong and able woman came to the theater's rescue just a year after Winslow's death and in the process set in motion a system that dictated the theater's operation almost to this day. Once, when asked about a woman's place in society, the new owner, Elizabeth Baker, said: "Every human being has a first duty to himself or herself. We must find our inner powers…to find expression for ourselves, our thoughts and feelings. This may take many and various forms, from pottery to politics, but it is only a matter of courage, to dare to be ourselves, to dare to do, to dare to try our wings."

Baker, whose husband, John, was president of Ohio University, saw an opportunity to offer advanced dramatic arts students invaluable practical training while at the same time ensuring that the theater had a company-in-residence every summer. That system has continued almost to the present, with a new crop of acolytes coming to Chatham every summer to take up residence in the one-time manse turned dormitory and practice every element of their craft, including acting technique and set and costume design. Each summer saw a roster of guest artists, typically including artists with résumés including work in film, TV and/or the New York stage.

In those early years of the company-in-residence system, Baker partnered with Ohio University, which became the lessee of the property, essentially creating an extension of the university's theater program. Serving as executive director was Christopher Lane, who taught at the university and in the summer months had suffered through the almost unbearable heat of southeastern Ohio as director of the Ohio Valley Summer Theatre. (Like so many before him, he was attracted to the cool summer breezes and fertile cultural soil of Cape Cod.) Baker also directed plays throughout the years and particularly gravitated to O'Neill's works.

Lane directed the Monomoy program for twenty-two years until he and his wife, Charlotte, retired in 1979. (Charlotte was another strong woman who proved integral to the growth of the Monomoy program. Sadly, she and Christopher were killed in an automobile accident in 1982.) At that point, Ohio University brought on as director Alan Rust, who had worked for several years with Lane at Monomoy. Rust says of his tenure at the theater, "I said I'd do it for five years and I've been here thirty-nine."

In recent years, the summer company-in-residence had come from the University of Hartford's Hartt School Division of Theatre, where Rust is now division director. But just like their earlier counterparts from Ohio University, they "lived every aspect of theater from 8 a.m. to midnight" every day of the summer, says Rust. And, just as in the past, there is a uniquely varied menu of performances. In fact, as longtime Chatham resident and

Monomoy Theatre, *110 in the Shade*, 2017. *Michael and Suz Karchmer.*

actor Julie Harris wrote in an introduction to Davis's book, "I was aware that right down Main Street in Chatham was the Monomoy Theatre, where I could see a summer season of plays, a musical, and a Shakespearean drama or comedy included."

Note: Following determination of safety violations on the theater property by the Chatham Board of Health in 2018, there was disagreement about who should pay for repairs between the University of Hartford and the longtime property owners, the Steindler Trust. Kathi Scrizzi Driscoll outlined the result of that disagreement in a January 4, 2020 article in the *Cape Cod Times*.

> *The training program for college students—which produced eight shows in 10 summer weeks—went dark for the first time in 60 years in 2019, after the Main Street property that the program had long leased was to be sold to Newton developer/part-time town resident Greg Clark.*
>
> *Now working as Chatham Productions LLC, Clark, founder of Alexandra Construction in Newton Upper Falls, officially bought the property at 776 Main St. and 70 Depot Road in September for $3.65 million.*
>
> *Clark first unveiled his preliminary future plans in a late-November [2019] preapplication conference with the town's Historic Business*

District Commission, and members did a site visit a few days later. Plans included restoring and expanding the theater complex—as well as putting ten two-story buildings for over-55 housing on the back portion of the land.

At this writing (March 2020), building plans also include a restaurant, retail space related to the theater and new student housing. Clark has made it clear, according to Driscoll's article, that "he wants to save the main historic theater buildings and continue their cultural use." The Friends of Monomoy, a group of community members supporting the theater, have been "cautiously optimistic," according to the article, that renovations will soon be complete and the curtain will once again rise on the venerable property's stage. In the meantime, the group is planning to stage shows for the 2020 summer season at various venues in the town.

The Chatham Drama Guild: From Church Basement to Home of Its Own

As noted in the previous section, it was in 1931 that the Chatham Drama Guild came together as a group. According to inveterate Cape theater historian Evelyn Lawson in her 1969 book *Theater on Cape Cod*, fifteen locals gathered in the basement of the Chatham Methodist Church "for the purpose of inducing a greater interest in the spoken drama and a closer feeling of sociability in Chatham and neighboring towns." In other words, from the very beginning, the theater was organized as a community theater with a commitment to working with talented amateurs at its core.

According to Scott Hamilton, longtime Guild member and current treasurer, the commitment remains to this day, despite the rigors of making ends meet in the present day. "A lot of theaters in the area are bringing in professionals, both onstage and as technicians. We've avoided that and tried to stay true to our original mission. That doesn't always make it easy to compete when you're surrounded by companies bringing in pros," he says.

Still, the Guild has survived for almost ninety years, through all kinds of conditions. It is, in fact, the archetypical family theater, with one generation after another of local families adding their names to cast lists and serving on the board.

In the beginning, the group performed in church basements and found spaces. Then, in 1934, it moved operations over to Harold Dunbar's arts center/converted toy factory, eventually to become Monomoy Theatre. In fact, as noted earlier, the group was so intimately associated with the old building that the theater was dubbed the Guildhouse.

When successive Monomoy owners Winslow and Baker began bringing in companies of professionals for the summer season, the Guild was generally limited to using the space in the off-season. This was something of a trial, because the old building was unheated. So, the group often mounted productions in the town's former high school, which for years was the only heated stage in Chatham.

As a kickoff to an invigorated postwar era, in 1947, the Guild graced the Monomoy stage with a production of the comedy classic *Arsenic and Old Lace*. According to author and historian Lawson—who was also a noted drama critic, "It was a smash hit, which stimulated an increase in membership and a yearly schedule of three plays each season and numerous one-act, workshop plays." (The group still mounts three productions a year—with major productions in the spring and fall and a slightly less ambitious production in the busy summer months. And in an effort to economize, it closes up shop in the off-season months of January, February and March.)

In the 1950s, with a growing membership and an organization to run, the Guild determined it needed a home of its own; it was no longer feasible to meet in local inns and churches. So, thanks to a donation of land from longtime Cape merchant Nickerson Company, the Guild had a plot of land in Chatham and building materials from a longtime member's demolished building. This is just one more example of the consistent community support that has been an important contributor to the development of the theater culture across Cape Cod.

For twenty years, the group held business meetings and social events at its new hall, continuing to mount productions at Monomoy. Along with its own productions, the group often supplied onstage and technical talent to round out the company-in-residence. (As should become clear in these pages, the Cape's theater history is full of instances of groups working together and sharing talent to mount productions.) Some

Vintage Chatham Drama Guild poster. *Author's collection.*

of its own productions from that period include *Barefoot in the Park*, *Desk Set*, *Send Me No Flowers*, *Mr. Roberts* and the classic *Inherit the Wind*, which will forever be associated with Spencer Tracy and the 1960 film version. Then, in 1976, the group enlarged and renovated its headquarters to include a stage of its own. That meant it could finally stage its own productions on the schedule that best suited its own members. And in early 2018, the group completed another renovation to the hall, fortifying and reducing the height of the stage for safety reasons and doing a general update of the building and facilities.

As testimony to the Guild's long history, its hall/theater complex is filled with posters from past productions. Recent productions have included *Seussical the Musical* in the summer of 2018, *The Miracle Worker* in May 2018, *Mary Poppins* in 2017 and *Beauty and the Beast* in 2016. And the Guild's Hamilton notes that, over the years, there have been repeat performances of some perennial audience-pleasers. For example, they've mounted the ever-popular musical/love story *Guys and Dolls* three times in their history.

It's really not surprising that amateur, community theaters like the Guild turn to sure bets for at least parts of their seasons, when they are

Chatham Drama Guild stage. *Author's collection.*

Chatham Drama Guild, *Beauty and the Beast*, 2016. *Michael and Suz Karchmer.*

dependent on ticket sales for such a large portion of their income. (As Hamilton notes, "You can always count on a Rodgers and Hammerstein.") But like other groups on the Cape, the Guild is determined to add thought-provoking shows to its mix, hence the May 2018 production of *The Miracle Worker*.

According to Hamilton, a partnership with one of the other groups in the area may be in the Guild's future. If that happens, it will be an extension of the cooperative spirit that companies on Cape Cod in general—and in Chatham in particular—have shown for nearly a century.

Cape Cod Theatre Company/Home of the Harwich Junior Theatre: Incubator for Theater Talent

Ask almost any longtime actor, director or theater technician on Cape Cod where they got their start, and they'll tell you, simply, "Harwich." And that's just the beginning. Harwich alums can be found on the Great White Way, in Hollywood, in long-running TV shows and even in Cirque du Soleil. Through all of its almost seventy years (at this printing), Cape Cod Theatre Company in Harwich, previously the Harwich Junior

Theatre, has been a smooth-running machine, taking the raw material of youthful energy and talent and turning it into a wellspring of professional talent—to say nothing of a constant stream of professional-quality productions.

In the words of producing artistic director Nina Schuessler, "We are an incubator for talent. We like to think of our organization as a family, and many of our family members have transformed their experience here into careers in the arts. And others have applied the confidence and skills they gained at the Cape Cod Theatre Company to highly successful careers in business, as teachers, and in government. In either case, their work with us has been a transformational experience."

The small-town New England feel of Harwich, with its quaint, often-classic buildings and picturesque harbors, would seem to make it an unlikely spot for Cape Cod's "talent central." But in the middle of the last century, founder Betty Bobp, already a noted drama teacher at Boston's Wheelock College, saw the potential of Harwich's ancient, four-story Exchange Hall, at that time the tallest building on Cape Cod. The first Exchange Hall was built in 1855, and longtime residents still tell stories of its agricultural fairs with livestock on the premises. That first structure burned in 1876 and was replaced six years later. A 2017 article, "The Harwich Exchange Building: It Was a Community Cornerstone," in the *Annual Guide* of *Cape Cod Life*, describes the updated structure.

> *Measuring fifty-eight by one hundred feet, this mercantile exchange housed retail space, a post office, and town offices on the ground floor; an eight hundred–seat auditorium with a full performance stage on the second floor; and an octagonal roller-skating rink on the third floor, complete with a bandbox above. The fourth floor was an attic space, with a ladder leading to a cupola tower that was used to watch for fires and to spot enemy planes during World War II. It is said that sailors traveling in Nantucket Sound could view the tower and used it as a guidepost. The massive cellar could store 5,000 barrels of cranberries for seasonal shipment, and in later years the local police used a portion of the space for a shooting range.*

Bobp was attracted not only to the performance stage but also to the space for teaching and implementing every aspect of theater, including acting, directing, set design and construction, prop creation, costume design and playwriting. In 1951, she secured space in the building, and by the next year,

Cape Cod Theatre Company/ Home of the Harwich Junior Theatre founder Betty Bobp (*far right*) instructing young actors, circa 1955. *Bob Place Photography*.

Bobp and a few volunteers were ready to mount productions. That season featured *Cinderella*, *Tom Sawyer* and *The Ghost of Mr. Penny*.

According to the theater's online history, "Betty made the costumes, taught the students, built the sets, and directed the three shows on a budget

HARWICH JUNIOR THEATRE

PRESENTS

THE SLEEPING BEAUTY

by

Charlotte B. Chorpenning

Sponsored by Harwich Recreation Council - Third Season

HARWICH EXCHANGE HALL

Tuesday, July 6 - 8:00 P.M.   Thursday, July 8, - 8:00 P.M.

Left: Cape Cod Theatre Company/ Home of the Harwich Junior Theatre, vintage program. *Courtesy Barb Cahoon.*

Below: Cape Cod Theatre Company/ Home of the Harwich Junior Theatre, *Beauty and the Beast*, 1959. *Bob Place Photography.*

of just $100. The organization's following began to take hold, and a fourth summer production was added to the roster beginning in 1954."

Then, in 1959, the Harwich Junior Theatre was incorporated, and the 1960s ushered in two programs that have remained lynchpins of the theater to this day: an apprentice program and a youth touring company called the Junior Players. From the beginning, the theater's culture has focused on identifying and nurturing creativity in young people.

"When you work with children you find that they are filled with creativity. If you give them the chance and nurture the kernel of creativity, it just naturally comes out onstage. There's a lot adults can learn from the way young people just naturally reflect the drama in life. In fact, our founder saw children as co-creators of the work we do," Schuessler says.

In 1965, the Exchange Hall was scheduled for demolition, so it became clear that the theater needed a new home. At that point, Bobp moved the organization to its current location in the former Ocean Hall in West Harwich.

During that period, the theater established one of many artistic collaborations that cemented its reputation as a nexus of children's theater. Harwich summer resident Aurand Harris, a well-known and prolific playwright for young audiences, used the theater as a testing ground for new material. He worked with the theater to produce shows on the Harwich stage before publication. For example, his successful *Rags to Riches*, which spins the tale of a dime-novel hero who rises from "rags to riches," premiered on the new Harwich Junior Theatre stage in 1966.

The next couple of decades saw moves to expand the theater's influence, both into the Cape's off-season and outward geographically. In 1970, Junior Theatre alums Susan Kosoff and Jane Staab, along with Anthony Hancock, established the Harwich Winter Theatre. And in the late 1970s, Schuessler, along with noted Cape performers Sherrie and Phillip Scudder, formed the Helikon Theatre, which produced ten shows in the nine off-season months, while Bobp's Harwich Junior Theatre productions continued to run during the summer months of June, July and August. Then, in 1981, Staab and Kosoff—who, along with Bobp, were professors at Wheelock College—co-founded the Wheelock Family Theatre. (See Closeup interview with Kosoff.)

Founder Betty Bobp remained an advisor to the theater into the 1990s, with Schuessler coming on as full-time producing artistic director in 1996. That next year, Bobp passed away, but not before passing on the theater's torch to her protégé.

Above: Cape Cod Theatre Company/Home of the Harwich Junior Theatre, Ocean Hall. *Courtesy Barb Cahoon.*

Left: Cape Cod Theatre Company/Home of the Harwich Junior Theatre, *Androcles and the Lion*, 1968. *Bob Place Photography.*

Schuessler describes a scene that seems straight from a dramatist's pen. "I was there at her bedside and she asked me to promise to continue my commitment to the theater. So, through the years we've tried to follow her lead and make the theater an inclusive community for both children and adults. And, in the process, we're transforming lives."

In 1997, the theater was rewarded for its efforts with a regional award for excellence and achievement in theater from the New England Theatre Conference. Then, in 2006, the theater opened its Arts Center, expanding its rehearsal, classroom and performance space, bolstering its ability to spread its influence across the region. Nine years later, the organization changed its name to Cape Cod Theatre Company/Home of the Harwich Junior Theatre, as if in recognition of its growing influence. By then, the theater had evolved from a small, seasonal venture to a year-round center for theater arts education and outreach—and a semiprofessional theater that mounts ten full-scale productions each year for audiences of more than twenty thousand. (Seasoned theater professionals and members of the Actors' Equity Association regularly staff productions and classrooms, lending experience in specific aspects of theater, including directing; acting; choreography; sound, lighting, and set design; playwriting; and music.) Still, Schuessler says the new name intentionally maintains the reference to its significant Harwich Junior Theatre roots and history.

Like other regional theater directors, Schuessler talks about the financial challenges of providing performances and arts education. But if the past is a predictor, Harwich is destined to remain a center for theater on Cape Cod.

Closeup: Sue Kosoff

When writer and director Susan Kosoff talks about her mentor, Betty Bobp, she says the CCTC founder "had theater in her bones. I've never known anyone who knew more about theater—from staging shows with ultimate creativity, to bringing out the best in everyone on stage. And there was absolutely no one like her when it came to working with children. No one. She was always a teacher at-heart."

Kosoff first came to the Harwich theater as a twenty-year-old apprentice back in 1964, when she was a student of Bobp's at Boston's Wheelock College. "I've never known anyone who lived more for theater than Betty; she spent every free minute at the theater. In fact, she once admonished me for not being at the theater during a free period."

By the next summer, Kosoff was serving as assistant to the producer in Harwich. By the year after that, she began a five-year stint as producer.

For a few years in the 1970s, she was a founding member of the Harwich Winter Theatre, which focused attention on adult productions, rather than the family fare at its big sister. But the financial climate was unkind in the 1970s, and the group found it hard to keep the books balanced. After five years, it disbanded. "Luckily, I had a 'day job' teaching at Wheelock, so I was able to go back to that," she says. In fact, both she and Harwich alum Jane

Cape Cod Theatre Company/Home of the Harwich Junior Theatre, *Wind in the Willows*, 1969. *Bob Place Photography.*

Staab taught at the college, where the duo founded the Wheelock Family Theatre in 1981, along with Anthony Hancock and Andrea Gesner. Now the Boston University Wheelock Family Theatre, the company is noted in the area for its stunning, often lavish productions of both children's classics and musicals, along with thought-provoking dramas like *To Kill a Mockingbird*.

In fact, Kosoff was at Wheelock for thirty-one years before retiring and finding her way back to the Cape full-time. But through those three decades, she stayed involved with the Harwich theater, serving on its board and contributing both writing and directing skills. "It was writing that drew me to the theater in the first place, so I'm always open to new writing projects," she says. And she ticks off a number of projects, including adaptations of *The Little Prince* and *The Secret Garden*.

If writing drew her to the theater, it was the unique character of life on Cape Cod that brought her back to the peninsula. "There's something about the Cape that just brings you back; it's a feeling of home you just don't find anywhere else. And there's that same feeling about theater. Being part of it for all these years gives me a sense of history—a feeling of continuance."

She tells the story of a trip she and Staab made a few years ago, coming back from a stint working on a production in New York. They stopped for lunch at a restaurant along the highway, and as they munched on sandwiches, a man came over to the table to say hello. "It was someone who had been one of our apprentices years ago, and there he was in the same restaurant in New York! It's just amazing how circular the theater world is."

And the "sense of home" is particularly strong at the Harwich theater, where, she says, there is a "welcoming atmosphere. It's really more collegial than competitive; I never get the feeling anyone feels threatened [by another artist]."

These days, you're apt to find Kosoff at the theater during rehearsals for a play she's either written or is directing (sometimes both). Clearly, she has come home.

The Cape Cod Repertory Theatre: Bringing the World to Cape Cod Bay

The Cape Cod Repertory Theatre, a professional, non-Equity company situated in the small bayside town of Brewster, calls itself, according to its online history "an artist-driven company committed to providing professional creative opportunities for the artists of our community, wonderfully talented people who choose to make their homes right here on Cape Cod."

Toward that end, in its history, the group says it brings in professionals "from the wider world of theater to work with us, and so we are able to produce a great variety of stories with a growing family of artists." The theater's history continues:

> We place value on the art of theater and appreciate its importance in the lives of both our artists and our audiences. We think this makes for a dynamic, eclectic organization with art at its center. We are a company dedicated to great stories. We read and read and read some more, all in an effort to choose plays and musicals that speak to us for our time. We commission new work, often written by local playwrights, and then we produce it—stories you've never seen before, sparked from the imaginations of the collaborators involved.

In a July 25, 2018 article in *Cape and Plymouth Business*, producing artistic director Janine Perry said, "Bringing in outside talent keeps us from becoming myopic. We don't want to lose that connection to the outside world."

Founded in 1986, the theater came to Brewster in 1992, taking over what used to be a kids' summer camp, Camp Monomoy. The company produces four to five plays during the indoor theater season (May through December). In the summer, it offers professional shows for children in its outdoor theater. The company is definitely one of the Cape's success stories, with annual attendance just over twenty thousand and a subscription base of nine hundred. Making these figures even more impressive, Perry points out in the *Cape and Plymouth Business* article that it's often challenging to make ends meet in the theater world. "If you're involved in the arts in this country, you're always living on the edge," she says.

The group declares in its history:

> *The company has worked hard to choose plays and musicals that continually challenge the artists who work here whether those artists are actors, designers, directors or technicians. We want to work with the best theater we can find. Often our choices are works that may not ordinarily be produced because we try not to let size of cast, degree of difficulty, or relative obscurity step in the way of choosing a show. And, most importantly, we have and will continue to produce new work.*

A look at a typical season offers a window into the company's productions. In 2015, the Rep offered the following:

> *Failure: A Love Story: A quirky comic love story set in 1928 and featuring the line, "Upon entering the United States, the first order of business for Heiner and Marishka Failbottom was to have their bottoms chopped off by an overzealous Ellis Island desk clerk."*
> *Outside Mullingar: A contemporary romantic comedy set in the Irish countryside.*
> *Evita: The popular musical about Argentina's first lady, Eva Peron.*
> *Mr. Burns, a Post-Electric Play: A look at the importance of art after an apocalyptic event results in a world with no electricity.*
> *La Cage Aux Folles: The Tony Award–winning and hilarious look at one family's attempt to appear "normal" to the in-laws.*
> *Elephant and Piggie's "We are in a play": A children's musical experience taken from the pages of Mo Willems's award-winning, best-selling children's books*
> *Footlight Fantasies on the Road: Billed as a fun fundraiser.*

Like so many Cape Cod theaters, the company does have an educational arm, with classes in acting, directing and playwriting and master classes in specific areas of theater. It also maintains an internship program, where local artists are mentored by gust directors and the artistic staff. Local playwrights' work and pieces dealing with local issues are often showcased at the Brewster center.

For example, in 2017, the company presented a work titled *Boundless*, a play that serves as a dramatic and musical exploration of the lives of struggling fishermen on Cape Cod. Longtime Cape Rep members and playwrights Alison Weller and Damien Baldet interviewed fishermen and their families, local politicians, scientists and suppliers to produce the ingredients for the work. In fact, the show is actually part of a larger project, the Cape Cod Fishing Project, aimed at shining a light on the often difficult lives of local fishing families.

The company also operates an outreach program, which features company members in musical revues at senior centers, libraries and nursing homes across the Cape.

A note: The company views its mission as twofold. Along with mounting several productions per year, it is committed to restoring and rehabilitating the historic property within Nickerson State Park, including four structures that have become the lynchpins in the group's Brewster campus. Below is a description of those projects, taken from the group's website (www.caperep.org).

> *The Indoor Theater was built in 1959 and used as a dining hall by Camp Monomoy. The company opened this 129-seat theater in 1997 and now operate a five-play indoor theater subscription season from May through early December in the space.* [Note: The theater has an impressive 900-person subscriber base, who reliably make up 30 percent of ticket sales.]
>
> *The Outdoor Theater. The group rehabilitated this structure in 1992 with the help of Edward Bangs Kelley and Elza Kelley Foundation. It has been the scene of everything from Shakespeare to Agatha Christie. The company also uses the space to produce children's shows during the summer months.*
>
> *The Cape House, at the entrance of Route 6A, has sections that date to 1790. The camp used it to house summer employees and in 2010 the theater reclaimed the historic structure, using funds from a variety of grants to restore it into housing for both local and visiting artists, with a community room for rehearsing, performing and teaching classes in acting, directing and playwriting. According to the theater's history, "We now have a home for creativity and have preserved an historic structure for future generations to enjoy."*

> *The Barn, which was built in the late 19th century, sits behind the Cape House on Route 6A. The restored space has been renovated and is being used to expand programming in performance, education, and community-building.*

On its website, the company expresses its mission in these words:

> *Whether on stage or off, our journey is and will continue to be, down roads to epic adventure, to places we have never been, with people we have never met, experiencing situations and moral dilemmas that we know in our heart will always connect us across time and space to the rest of humanity. Remnants of times and people past will always exist here to remind us that we are connected, that we come from a past, live in the present and bequeath a future, that we need to contribute not just possess, to create not just consume.*

Moving on to the Mid-Cape, often seen as the Cape's business center, there are a number of theaters with long, continuing histories. In fact, one, the Cape Playhouse in Dennis, holds the distinction as the oldest continually operating professional summer playhouse in the United States. So to continue our beachcombing…

5

IN THE MIDDLE OF IT ALL

THEATER IN THE MID-CAPE AREA

Long histories, solid theatrical traditions and associations with internationally renowned theatrical figures define the theaters in the Mid-Cape area. From the Cape Playhouse to the Melody Tent to the nearly one-hundred-year-old Barnstable Comedy Club, the theaters are an integral part of life in their towns. Here's a look at the histories of the theaters that dot the Mid-Cape area.

ALMOST ONE HUNDRED YEARS IN BARNSTABLE

The Barnstable Village Hall sits on Route 6A in the quaint and historic Barnstable Village. The hall was built in 1912 and just a decade later became the site of the Barnstable Comedy Club's very first production, with the group mounting its productions on the Village Hall stage to this day. In its history, the group calls the BCC a "mixture of small-town tradition and soaring aspiration," qualities that seem evident in its genesis. In fact, the company—still all-volunteer to the present—is the oldest live community theater on Cape Cod and one of the oldest in the country.

In its written history, the theater makes it clear that it differs from some of its neighbors—the Cape Playhouse and the Melody Tent (both targeting the Cape's multitude of summer visitors), for example—in its role as an integral part of the year-round community. It all began back in 1922, when theater enthusiast and innkeeper Joe Turpin hosted a meeting of like-minded residents at his Old Barnstable Inn. At that first meeting, plans were fleshed out for the group's first production, *Lady Windermere's Fan*, which was mounted on the Village Hall stage on April 1, 1922. The name "Barnstable Comedy Club" was printed on the tickets for that first show, with reserved seats going for a whopping seventy-five cents (including a war tax).

It seems that Mid-Cape audiences were more than ready to leave behind the war-weary years of the previous decade for a little light entertainment. In fact, the show was so successful that the original group of thespians took it on the road to another five locations on the Cape. For a few years, the group's schedule was nothing if not irregular. Members rehearsed at the Inn and in private homes, including that of longtime theater buff and community activist Mary Mortimer, mounting plays when the spirit moved and they could find available venues. Mortimer was the director of that very first play and remained active in the group for decades after. This plotline is repeated again and again in Cape Cod theater groups, where members—and their children and grandchildren—stay involved throughout their lives.

A perfect example of that phenomenon is Ann Ring, who thought it might be fun to help out with a production of *The King and I* in 1976 and got hooked by the BCC bug. She has since performed in, directed and produced myriad productions, along with serving as business manager. "Being part of a production is incredibly creative and I don't think there's anything more rewarding. Whether it's helping an actor find the right emphasis onstage or mixing up the right makeup to look like blood under the lights, it's all about being inventive," she said in an interview in the comfortable-if-ancient Village Hall.

Back in the history books, during the late twenties and early thirties, the group operated as an arm of the Barnstable Women's Club, which held the keys to the Town Hall. In 1933, the group decided to go back to using its original name, with its published intent "to produce plays for any organization willing to sponsor and help sell tickets, to help improve the stage at the Village Hall." But, of course, these were the years of the Great Depression, so it was often impossible even to break even on production costs. (In fact, theater legend has it that the bags of fudge that sold for a dime each sometimes made more money than the BCC shows themselves.)

One way the group dealt with the stranglehold of the Depression during that period was to join forces with the Chatham Drama Guild and the Woods Hole Theatre Company. The group performed three one-acts and one full-length production, then determined that the logistics involved in sharing talent and sets made the arrangement untenable.

Barnstable Comedy Club, early production of *The Mikado*. *Courtesy of BCC staff.*

So the group went solo for a few years, until closing up shop through the war years—like most theaters on Cape Cod. The curtain rose again at the Barnstable Town Hall in 1946, and through the late forties and into the fifties the group mounted two or three productions a year. In 1959, the company was lucky enough to attract the attention of a dancer and teacher who was to teach the women of BCC how to truly soar across a stage. In the process, La Meri (Russell Meriwhether Hughes) created an ethnic dance group.

Here is what she wrote in her book *Dance Out the Answer*, about her first encounter with the group.

> *I began giving exercise classes gratis for this organization. Of course, I could not leave it at that. I had five talented young dancers studying with me in the daytime, so, theater-minded me, I had to put on a full-length production with five good amateurs and a dozen ladies who had never danced before in their lives. It took all winter, for I made all the costumes myself, but we built an audience for ethnic dance.*

In 1961, the group was finally in the position to buy the Village Hall from the Barnstable Women's Club, giving it a permanent home of its own. For the first time, the group was rooted to the community not just through sentiment, but in fact. However, as all homeowners know, owning your own piece of property is a double-edged sword; suddenly you have expenses you never dreamed of. So, after making the purchase, the group punched up its

83

Barnstable Comedy Club, vintage stage production. *Courtesy of BCC staff.*

level of activity, sometimes offering as many as ten or twelve performances of a single production in an effort to capitalize on ticket sales.

In the heady period just after the purchase, the group began an association with one of the great names in American letters, Kurt Vonnegut Jr., who had a home in the area. In fact, the Hall was the site of premieres of two of his plays—*My Name Is Everyone* and *Epicac* in the 1960s. And Vonnegut—who agreed to waive royalty fees for the group on any of his work—did a stint as president of the organization. (This is another theme that plays out again and again in the Cape theater world, as internationally renowned celebs who summer on the Cape become part of the Cape theater community. Vonnegut was also an ardent supporter of the Arena Theatre in Orleans.)

These days, the group produces four main shows per season, which include a musical and three plays beginning in November through May. For example, for the 2018–19 season, the group offered *Grease* as its fall musical, an original play, *Lettice and Lovage*, *The 1940s Radio Hour* and *Calendar Girls*. Its annual calendar also includes a slate of special events such as the Annual Barnstable Village Stroll, staged readings and acting and directing

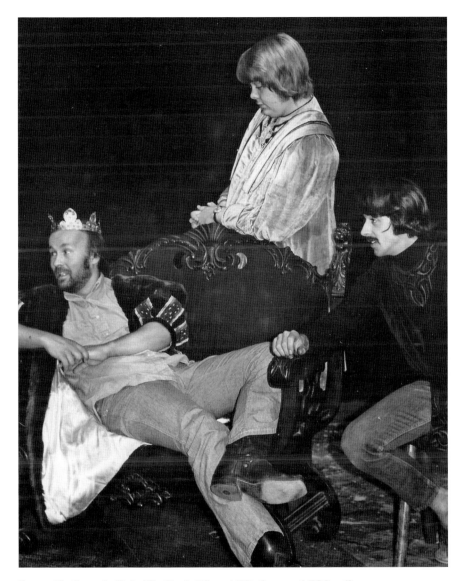

Barnstable Comedy Club, *The Lion in Winter*, 1972. *Courtesy of BCC staff.*

workshops. And, in an effort to make financial ends meet, the group rents the space out to other theater groups and for private functions.

"It's not always easy to survive as a community theater, but we are committed to continuing the work we do—creating a make-believe world for both audiences and performers. We'll definitely be around for our 100th anniversary," says Ring.

The Cape Playhouse—America's Oldest Professional Summer Theater

One thing that should be clear about the Cape Cod theater world is that—just as in any play—the same characters show up again and again. So it should probably be no surprise that someone who was deeply involved in the very beginnings of theater on the Cape—and American theater at large—would turn up in another locale on the Cape.

That was the case with Raymond Moore, whose experience with—and influence on—Cape theater began where it all started, in Provincetown. Moore showed up in town just as one segment of the original Provincetown Players had made its way to Frank Shay's barn, creating the Barnstormers. Originally, Moore had come to the tip of Cape Cod to paint. Like so many visual artists, he had come for the unique Cape Cod light. But by the early 1920s, he was also trying his hand at playwriting, with one of his early works showing up on the Barnstormers roster. But, as we noted in our earlier discussion of the group in Shay's barn, infighting eventually led to the group's demise. For one season in the mid-twenties, Moore and partner Harold Winston took over the barn and brought in an acting company for a season.

But Moore had other plans and another locale in mind for the future. He was aware that, although Provincetown was—for a time at least—the center of theater on Cape Cod, it was hardly the center of the Cape. He knew that, for a theater to be a commercial success, it really needed to be situated closer to both Boston and the affluent towns of Osterville and Cotuit. So he cast his gaze on the Mid-Cape area and spent many days wandering around the area looking for just the right site for a new—hopefully commercially successful—theater. Of course, he was just a poor player trying to make ends meet at the tip of the Cape, so it took him time to gather the resources necessary to make a move up-Cape possible.

The right site—and the perfect building for his needs—seemed to be waiting for Moore in Dennis Village. The building, the old Nobscussett Meetinghouse—originally built in 1790—had had several incarnations until ending up as a barn and slaughterhouse at about the turn of the century. It seemed to be just waiting for Moore to give it a new—and this time enduring—life. (Theater legend has it that Moore was actually able to purchase the building for the then-princely sum of $200.)

But first Moore had to find the right site, one that would allow for growth and actually create a theater campus in Dennis Village. Moore found just

The Cape Playhouse, one of Cape Cod's historic theaters. *Author's collection.*

that in a three-acre parcel of land just off the Old King's Highway (now the Cape's historic Route 6A). At that point in Cape Cod history, it was common practice to move buildings from place to place, and Moore hired what was then the premier area company to undertake the task. There was one small problem, however: Moore ran out of funds before he could pay the firm the full price, so the building was transported just part of the way to the newly purchased parcel of land, then unceremoniously dumped at the roadside, where it sat until Moore finally resuscitated his finances and was able to pay the remaining balance to the contractor.

Finally, the building was situated on its site and renovated by a distinguished theater architect and theater designer hailing from New York, Cleon Throckmorton.

Author Marcia Monbleau writes in her book *The Cape Playhouse*:

> *Throckmorton, showing considerable respect for the old structure, turned it into a theater while preserving much of its ecclesiastical appearance. A substantial addition to the north end provided space for a fly gallery, stage and proscenium. The dark oak pews were retained for orchestra seats, and*

the church's hand-hewn beams, joined by wooden pegs, were not improved on by the careful, thoughtful designer.

So now all that was left for Moore to do was to come up with the funds to complete the project—which had quickly become a money pit—and find performers for the upcoming season. Somehow, he managed to come up with the funds to allow him to go ahead with plans for the first season, 1927. It may have been the language he used in his mailing to potential patrons in the Mid-Cape area that convinced them to open their wallets. He was nothing if not prescient when, according to Evelyn Lawson in her book *Theater on Cape Cod*, he wrote,

> *The Cape Playhouse hopes to stand for the best in the field of art, and to establish something infinitely more important than a commercial theater. It hopes to be sincere in its efforts and sane in its management and membership. It hopes to offer the public something of definite value, and to receive in return the public's interest, cooperation, and financial support at the box office. It expects to meet its own expenses without appeals for subsidies from a tolerant public. It hopes to aid actors, artists, writers and musicians.*

And he was just as indomitable in his ability to bring in the talent he needed to populate the stage at his new playhouse. He even convinced the incomparable Basil Rathbone to join the troupe, with the star actually headlining four productions that summer. And Moore brought in other stars who—while not necessarily familiar to modern audiences—were Broadway luminaries at the time. They included Peggy Wood, Laura Hope Crews, Janet Beecher and Violet Kemble-Cooper.

That summer, the playhouse launched an ambitious nine productions, each one a resounding success, leading to financial success. (Here's a bit of theater trivia: According to Monbleau, on opening night, July 4, 1927, members of the audience watched the curtain rise on a glittering production of *The Guardsman* starring Basil Rathbone and Violet Kemble Cooper. When it rained, the roof leaked so badly that the audience put up umbrellas to protect their stylish theater outfits. Moore must have felt transported back to the first staging of the Provincetown Players' production of *Bound East for Cardiff* on that little theater on the wharf, when fog and drizzle filled the air around theatergoers.)

An astounding 98 percent of the subscribers signed on for another year, giving Moore the confidence he needed to move ahead with the next season.

Basil Rathbone and Nigel
Bruce as Holmes and Watson.
Sherlock Holmes Museum.

Monbelau notes that the playhouse has been called the "cradle of the stars," and that cradle began to rock in the season of 1928.

The distinguished-looking Robert Montgomery made his way to the Dennis stage for the last three productions of the year and—even more interestingly to today's audiences—two young actors made their first appearances on the stage that season: Henry Fonda and Bette Davis. It's now a part of theater legend that Davis had been ushering theatergoers to their seats just one week before being assigned a small part in a show, *Mr. Pim Passes By.* (Obviously, we now know that the *only* important thing about that unremarkable production was Davis's role in it.) According to Monbleau, apparently, Davis and her mother had trekked to Dennis in the hope that the young actor would manage to snare a position as an apprentice. When that didn't happen, she agreed to serve as an usher. And the rest, as they say, is history.

The success of the new enterprise meant that Moore had to shell out more money. Actors and technicians had to be housed, fed and paid, and, anyway, Moore had ambitions that went far beyond one mere summer theater; he was determined to create a true center for the arts in the Mid-Cape, including a "junior theater" for drama classes and an art gallery. So, whenever a piece of land nearby came up for sale, Moore was the first in line with cash in hand.

(Theories abounded about the source of his abundant funds, but no one—other than readers of the cheap romances popular at the time—could have guessed the source of his unending stream of dollars. More on that later.) The second building to be erected on the site was actually a set building for staging needed for shows. And, at about the same time, Moore invested in the gardens around the property that have since made it a horticultural destination.

The Wizard Comes to Dennis

It was 1930, and "talkies" were beginning to make their way onto screens across the country. An entrepreneur to the bone, Moore saw their potential and decided to build on the property a movie theater that was "artistic, intelligent and comfortable," according to Monbleau. (To this day, moviegoers at the Cape Cinema might use just those words to describe the theater.)

It was artistic: Architect Alfred Easton Poor (who had actually been part of the visual arts scene in Provincetown) designed the building to conform to local architectural style, using a Congregational church in nearby Centerville as a model. But it was the interior that was the real pièce de résistance. Moore brought in noted artist Rockwell Kent and collaborator Jo Mielziner to decorate the entire interior of the theater with a mural of the heavens that brings to mind some of the greatest works in classical European structures. While the Cinema mural differs in that it is modernistic in style, the sheer scope and majesty of the work brings to mind sites like the Sistine Chapel.

It was intelligent: Whenever Kent was asked about his creation, he said he designed it "to make people think," Monbleau writes. He certainly seems to have achieved his goal over the years, but so has the fare offered at the Cinema. Over the years, the theater has offered a range of new, experimental and foreign-language films. The very first film in 1930 was *With Byrd in the South Pole*, a world premiere. But the really big moment came nine years later, when MGM decided to use the Dennis site to test out its ambitious undertaking *The Wizard of Oz*. In a way, it made perfect sense for the studio to use the Cape screen for its debut; Margaret Hamilton had made her first professional appearance at the Cape Playhouse in the 1930s *Cape Cod Follies*. As Monbleau says in her book, "Now she was back, this time on the screen, with hooked nose and pale green face, threatening Dorothy and Toto and melting her way into American history."

It was comfortable: Moviegoers were treated to individual suede armchairs that had actually been designed by a local gallery. Of course, in these days of individual lounge chairs in theaters, that hardly seems the height of comfort. But at the time, it was considered most luxurious, and a recent renovation has brought seating more in line with modern standards.

So the Mid-Cape art colony was beginning to fill out, as it was filled with activity. There was of course the busy summer season at the main stage, children's shows both in the Junior Theatre and at various locales around the Cape and the movies and fabulous mural at the Cinema. Considering modest Cape standards, it was truly an empire. The peninsula was abuzz with theories about how Moore (a lowly Provincetown Player) could have amassed the fortune to build his colony. (Keep in mind that, once summer visitors depart, the Cape basically reverts to a small town where, to use the old expression, secrets are about as rare as hen's teeth.) As it turned out, Moore had been secretly married to one Edna Bradley Tweedy, an heiress who had graced him with hundreds of thousands of dollars over the years, really making the Cape Playhouse possible. And, upon Tweedy's death, a substantial sum from her estate made its way into the Playhouse's coffers.

But by the late 1930s, Moore—who was young by modern standards—seemed to be failing. There were rumors of a nervous breakdown or alcohol treatment in California, another short-term marriage, and he finally succumbed to a cerebral hemorrhage in 1940, at just forty-two.

A second golden era of theater on Cape Cod was about to begin. (The age of the Provincetown Players and Barnstormers at the tip of the Cape was certainly the first.)

Richard Aldrich and Gertrude Lawrence: At the Heart of Cape Theater History

Noted Broadway producer and business manager Richard Aldrich (originally from Boston and a Harvard graduate) had developed a reputation for turning failing theaters around and making them profitable. In fact, he had earned the nickname "theater doctor." As luck would have it, just as Moore was beginning to fail, he came in contact with Aldrich, who, in 1935, was co-managing a group of players that traveled through New England. By 1936, Aldrich was business manager of the Playhouse and, by 1938, producing director.

This was the beginning of what can only be termed a golden age in Cape theater history. Aldrich would go on to successfully manage four Cape theaters: the Cape Playhouse, the Melody Tent, the Falmouth Playhouse and the South Shore Music Circus. And his partner through it all was a noted star of the London and Broadway stages, Gertrude Lawrence, affectionately known to Cape Codders as "Mrs. A." Just look around the Cape and you see signs of her everywhere, from programs and photos from Cape Playhouse and Melody Tent productions to the stage that bears her name at the Dennis Union Church (now the site of productions by the Eventide Theatre Company. More on that group shortly.)

But when Lawrence came to Dennis in 1939, she had no intention of staying and taking up village life. Monbleau recounts the actress's first trip to the Cape. "Miss Lawrence came to the Cape on a rainy night in the summer of 1939, expecting nothing more than a one-week engagement at the Playhouse. She found, instead, the private life she had never known."

When Lawrence came to Dennis, she was already a big star and preceded by an impossible list of demands. But, just as in any old-fashioned melodrama, love found a way. By the following year, Aldrich and the star were married and Lawrence was ensconced as a hostess central to village life in Dennis.

But Lawrence and Aldrich were also an incredibly effective business team. Together, they instituted the "star system," bringing to all four of their theaters luminaries from stage and screen. The list includes Lillian Gish, Helen Hayes, Claudette Colbert, Eva Le Gallienne, Ezio Pinza and Roddy McDowall. And the big summer tents in Hyannis and Cohasset were actually the inspiration of Lawrence, based on a successful operation she'd seen in Florida. (More on that in the next section.)

And, of course, Lawrence was a fixture on the stage at the Playhouse beginning with her first performance there in *Private Lives* in 1940. According to Evelyn Lawson in her *Theater on Cape Cod*, "The star played the volatile Amanda, and it was said by some critics to have been her most enchanting role of the period."

The theater's audience continued to grow over the next few years, until World War II intervened. Like most theaters on the Cape, the Playhouse turned off the lights during the war years. But by the late forties, the theater was back up and running, and once again, the Aldriches were bringing in top talent from both coasts. But—as is all too often the case—real life can be as dramatic as theater. Gertrude Lawrence died in 1952, with her final role Anna in the Broadway production of *The King and I*.

A few years after his wife's death, Aldrich turned his attention to a new career in government; he was to become deputy director, then director, of the Foreign Operations Administration in Spain. He was succeeded at the Playhouse by Charles Mooney, who had originally come on the scene as an apprentice and worked his way up the theater's ladder, eventually becoming managing director. And, while he ascribed to his mentor's adherence to a "star system," he was taken by a new medium: television.

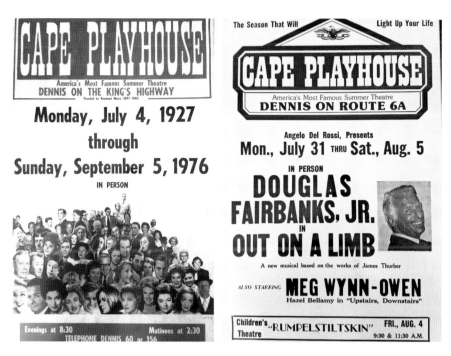

Left: The Cape Playhouse has always been known for its star power. *Author's collection.*

Right: Even stars from the silent-movie era performed at the Playhouse. *Author's collection.*

Before long, stars of the airwaves like Betsy Palmer, Orson Bean, George Gobel and Steve Allen were making appearances on the Playhouse stage. And, at the same time, the on-site theater school was feeding productions in Dennis and beyond. For example, way back in 1957, a student named Jane Fonda had a small part in a play titled *The Male Animal*, with the sixties seeing performances by students/soon-to-be-greats including Frank Langella and Danny DeVito.

As the years went by, productions at the theater continued to be star-driven and followed a time-honored formula that Moore had originally laid out. He said, according to Monbleau, "I try to give my patrons a well-rounded program, with one comedy, one mystery, one modern classic and one shocker on the schedule." For a while, his successors were able to book those choices through a circuit of stock theaters, COST (Council of Stock Theatres). The organization included the Westport County Playhouse in Westport, Connecticut; North Shore Music Circus in Beverly, Massachusetts; Ogunquit Summer Theatre in Ogunquit, Maine; and the Corning Summer Theatre in Corning, New York. But by the later years of the last decade, the circuit system no longer really existed, and subsequent directors at the Playhouse have had to find their own sources for productions.

Today, there are eleven buildings on the pastureland that Moore purchased almost one hundred years ago, including the newest addition, the Cape Cod Museum of Art. His dream of an art colony at the center of Cape Cod has been realized—in more ways than one. And the Cape Playhouse remains at the center of the complex.

To quote Monbleau as she closed her comprehensive history of the theater:

> As theaters go, the Playhouse isn't elegant, or large or well-to-do. It's a spare, old Yankee meetinghouse....But its walls have stories and the ghosts are grand. Shining stars and just-beginners have walked the stage. Their voices linger, and it doesn't take much imagination to picture them standing there still. The atmosphere is heavy with theater history and with history-in-the-making. The cradle still rocks.

In fact, the Playhouse seems like the perfect construct to serve as the "center" of theater on Cape Cod. It is alive with history, still attracts summer visitors—and performers—seeking a respite from summer heat and continues to live up to its promise to enthrall audiences again and again.

The Melody Tent

These days, the big tent in the west end of Hyannis is associated with popular musical acts. Every summer, the tent hosts a roster of performers in every musical category, ranging from Lynyrd Skynyrd to the Gipsy Kings and the Boston Pops. But that wasn't always the case. The Cape Cod Melody Tent actually has an illustrious past as a venue for summer theater. Along with its sister venue, the South Shore Music Circus, it became one of the first theatrical tents in the United States.

It all began in 1932, when Raymond Moore (as noted earlier, founder of the Cape Playhouse and an early member of the Provincetown Players) felt that he needed an additional site to stage his shows. From the beginning, the Playhouse attracted large crowds of summer theatergoers anxious to escape sweltering New York theaters, along with a cache of performers attracted to Cape Cod's coast.

Initially, Moore's search for more space led him up the coast to the South Shore community of Cohasset, where the historic old town hall seemed to be just waiting for him. That year, the venue featured performances from such luminaries as Humphrey Bogart, Josephine Hull and Van Heflin. The following year, Alexander Dean, then head of the drama department at Yale University and a noted figure in the theatrical world, formed the South Shore Players and continued the tradition of live performances in Cohasset, spotlighting such famous writers and actors as Edward Everett Horton, Arthur Treacher, Sylvia Sidney, Thornton Wilder and Sinclair Lewis. Even some unlikely celebs made their way to the old town hall.

For example, in his 2016 book about noted cartoonist Peter Arno, *Peter Arno: The Mad, Mad World of the* New Yorker's *Greatest Cartoonist*, Michael Maslin writes:

> *In midsummer of 1937 Arno deviated from his comfort zone and traveled out to Cohasset, Massachusetts, where he agreed to join—for just a week—the cast of the South Shore Players in a production of* Most of the Game, *a light comedy by John Van Druten, directed by noted Yale professor Alexander Dean. Arno's attorney said his client was taking a "theatrical vacation."*

By the end of the next decade, the size of the crowds far exceeded the ancient town hall's ability to accommodate them. The search began for a new venue that could handle the large summer crowds.

Enter Gertrude Lawrence and her husband, Richard Aldrich, whom we introduced in the earlier segment on the Cape Playhouse. As luck would have it, this was a time when tent theaters were beginning to operate on the East Coast, with the first in New Jersey and the second in Florida. Lawrence happened to see the tent in Florida—which was operated by a close friend, St. John Terrell, and set out to convince Richard that the tent concept was perfectly suited to New England in the summer. In her book *Theater on Cape Cod*, Evelyn Lawson recounts a conversation with one-time editor of the *Barnstable Patriot* Percy Williams, in which he describes Lawrence's campaign to locate a tent theater in New England.

> *She came back to New York and gave her husband and his associates glowing reports of Terrell's enterprise. She liked everything about the music-tent idea: the carnival atmosphere, the feeling of audience participation, the informality and the added dimension that acting and singing in-the-*

round afforded. The tent concept is a summer thing, you know, and she was a summer personality. "Everything that's light and gay!"…And most interesting of all to Aldrich and his backers, Miss Lawrence reported that Terrell's project was actually making money. The Florida people had accepted musicals offered in a circus atmosphere. And the shows were playing to packed houses, so why not a tent on Cape Cod?

(Actually, Lawrence and Aldrich originally approached the South Shore Players about the tent, but the Cohasset group passed on the idea at the time.)

So Lawrence turned her attention to Cape Cod. By the end of just one day spent searching on the Cape, she had found the perfect site, a whole block in Hyannis, that was to become the Cape Cod Music Circus, eventually renamed the Melody Tent. Opening night was July 4, 1950, which just happened to be Lawrence's birthday and the couple's tenth anniversary. That first night, the show at the circular theater was a musical, *The New Moon.*

In her account of the evening, Lawson describes the night's torrential rains, which almost swamped the orchestra. "The water poured under the back row of seats and cascaded down to form a pool in the orchestra pit that surrounded the round, raised stage. And as the orchestra rendered 'Lover Come Back to Me,' the rising waters all but engulfed the musicians and their instruments."

Vintage Melody Tent/Cape Cod Music Circus poster. *Courtesy Barb Cahoon.*

The damage was repaired, and the Circus went on to complete a season that included *The Merry Widow* and *Showboat*, both of which proved to be great hits. That set the tone for subsequent seasons, which were filled with new and popular musicals that would continue to feed the box office.

By the mid-fifties, traffic and lack of parking in downtown Hyannis dictated that the Circus pack up its tent and move. So, the tent was moved to its current site in the town's west end, with a capacity of 1,500. At the same time, the theater needed a new name, as another enterprise was claiming prior

Cape Cod Music Circus programs. *Courtesy Falmouth Museums on the Green.*

rights to Music Circus. Aldrich's publicist actually ran a contest to come up with a new name, with the theater critic for the *Cape Cod Standard Times*—then the Cape's daily paper—submitting the name that stuck.

Over the bridge in Cohasset, the South Shore Playhouse Associates was making progress of its own toward increasing its capacity to bring theater to summer visitors. At the end of 1950, the association announced that, on or about July 5, 1951, the group would begin presenting operettas and musical shows on the "horse grounds" of the Bancroft Estate in Cohasset. The production company would be known as the South Shore Music Circus Inc., and it brought Aldrich on board to manage and direct the productions in a musical tent seating one thousand people. This was actually the fourth enterprise to come under Aldrich's direction, joining the Melody Tent and the Falmouth Playhouse. (More on the Falmouth venue in the next chapter.)

The South Shore Music Circus became musical tent number four in the country. In anticipation of the upcoming performance season of 1951, the landscape of the Bancroft estate was modified to accommodate the tent. Horse stalls were torn down, buildings hauled away and new structures erected in their places. Interest in this new theater was so great that the first four performances of that season sold out in advance and the remaining three had near-capacity crowds. Tickets for that first season sold for $1.20 to $3.60 for the evening performances and $1.20 to $3.00 for the matinee on Thursday.

The list of stars from the early years of both the Melody Tent and Music Circus reads like a who's who of Hollywood and Broadway. Just for starters, the list included: Ginger Rogers, Douglas Fairbanks Jr., Angela Lansbury, Bob Hope, Helen O'Connell, Robert Merrill, Zero Mostel, Kitty Carlisle, Ann Miller, Jane Powell, Victor Borge, Debbie Reynolds, Benny Goodman, Dizzy Gillespie, Woody Herman, Rosemary Clooney, Pearl Bailey and John Raitt. The list could go on for pages. In fact, Aldrich became known for the star power he brought to all of his venues.

Here's an interesting piece of Cape Cod theater trivia: Bonnie Raitt, who often traveled with her dad, John, when he was on the road during summer months, has said that she feels like she grew up in the aisles of the Melody Tent. And, fittingly enough, she has often performed in the theater herself.

By the mid-fifties, Aldrich's theater career was coming to an end. As we noted in the segment on the Cape Playhouse, he opted for a new career in diplomacy. His attorney, David Holtzmann, bought the Tent and its property, continuing to mount popular musicals. And he added to the menu Sunday variety shows and jazz/big band concerts. All-time greats like Louis Armstrong, Duke Ellington, Stan Kenton, Dave Brubeck and Count Basie made their way to the Tent for the Sunday jam sessions.

As noted at the beginning of this segment, the Tent is now largely a music venue, with summer headliners including some of the greats in the music world. The property is now owned by the South Shore Playhouse Associates, which has brought the Tent into the modern era, with a series of improvements, including a state-of-the-art vinyl tent with cupola venting system, new seats, a new stage and computerized lighting and sound systems

It's interesting to note that, as a not-for-profit organization, the South Shore Playhouse Associates re-invests the profits from these two venues into other not-for-profit groups in the community. The organization has distributed over $3.7 million to such entities as the Cape Cod Conservatory/ Cape Cod Symphony Orchestra, the South Shore Conservatory, the Paul Pratt Memorial Library, South Shore Arts Center and the Arts Foundation of Cape Cod.

Eventide: In Memory of One of the Cape's Most Faithful Patrons

Noel Tipton is a musician by craft; he is a graduate of the noted Juilliard School and, along with his wife, operated a music school in Westfield, New Jersey, for thirty years. But he is also a great lover of theater. So, it's hardly surprising that when the founder of the Eventide Theatre Festival (which later became the Eventide Theatre Company) saw a chance to put the two together, he jumped at it.

In an interview in his Eastham home, which is filled with theater posters and memorabilia, he said, "I was interviewing for the job of choir director at the Dennis Union Church, and I saw that there was a perfect little stage in one of the church's rooms. I took the job specifically so I could fill the stage with the talent I saw all around me on the Cape. And when I saw the photo of Gertrude Lawrence in the church I thought, 'She had been such an important figure in the theater world, we just have to make use of her stage.'" (A side note: He was also intrigued by the fact that Anna Howard Shaw, a physician, leader of the suffrage movement in the nineteenth century and the first female minister to be ordained by the Methodist Church, had been the church's spiritual leader.)

Eventide poster. *Courtesy of Noel Tipton.*

It was in the late 1990s that Tipton first saw the church's Gertrude Lawrence Stage, which was built and named in 1954 in memory of Lawrence. Lawrence had played a key role in Cape Cod theater history, as we noted earlier in this chapter. In fact, she and husband Richard Aldrich, who managed no less than four major theaters on the Cape, were members of the church, which is almost literally a stone's throw away from the venerable Cape Playhouse. But it is worlds away in terms of focus.

From the beginning, it was Tipton's goal to bring community-based actors and "issue-related" programming to the stage, rather than the big-name stars and flashy productions that make up the Playhouse's fare. At the start, that meant mounting

99

Eventide, Gertrude Lawrence Stage. *Author's collection.*

skits—with some, not surprisingly, focusing on Shaw and Lawrence. And the first big hit was an original play about Lawrence, titled simply *G.*

Another famous summer resident who became a loyal Eventide supporter around the turn of the last century was Julie Harris, following a chance meeting with Tipton in line waiting for *Rhinoceros*, the very first offering of the Wellfleet Actors Theatre (WHAT). Almost from that moment on, Harris and Tipton became fast friends, with *The Belle of Amherst* star often doing readings at the Dennis theater and becoming a regular presence at theater events, nearly until her death in 2013.

Tipton tells a charming story about the love for Harris among a faithful group of Cape Cod songsters, the birds that frequented the actress's backyard feeders. "Julie loved birds, and they seemed to know it. Flocks of them came into her yard every day. And, according to her housekeeper, on the day she died the birds all stopped singing."

By the middle of the first decade of this century, the company was ready to move beyond skits and occasional readings to a more formal schedule. At that point, Ellis Baker, who boasts a long history of producing and directing productions, took the helm. The company began to operate as a more formal theater company—rather than a festival—presenting regular productions.

These days, the company presents three full-stage productions a year, along with staged readings, often as part of a series entitled Cape Cod Voices, along with a playwriting competition that features two staged readings and a songwriting competition that ends in a performance. (According to Toby Wilson, longtime Eventide member and onetime artistic director, a number of winners of the songwriting competition have gone on to careers in the music industry.)

Wilson says the company usually limits the size of casts and scope of productions because of the modest size of its theater (seating just one hundred), but every now and then the company takes on larger productions. Recent examples include *A Funny Thing Happened on the Way to the Forum* and *A Little Night Music*.

Wilson is a member of another one of those Cape Cod theater families at the heart of the ever-expanding Cape theater universe. In fact, his mother, Eileen, was an actress, playwright and co-founder of the Martha's Vineyard Playhouse. (More on her and the rest of the family in chapter 7.)

Wilson calls Eventide a "community theater," which—to his way of thinking at least—puts it squarely between amateur and professional theaters.

Eventide, *A Funny Thing Happened on the Way to the Forum. Bob Tucker Photography.*

"We pay everyone at least something through a production, so we're not strictly amateur," he says. And like so many others in community theaters, he says it's challenging to keep a company operating in the black. "You really need a great ticket operation, probably more than anything else," he says.

Wilson notes that his company's productions attract performers and techs from all over the Cape and beyond, and—in turn—Eventide company members often journey to other towns for just the right, juicy part. Maybe Eventide's fortunate, central location is part of the draw. Or maybe it's just that "it's a fluid theater community. You go where the best part is, no matter how far it is."

Tilden Arts Center at Cape Cod Community College: A Commitment to Education Through Performance

When most people think of Cape Cod, they see in their mind's eye miles of unsullied beaches, quaint cottages and the occasional ice cream or saltwater taffy stand. But in the village of West Barnstable, the Cape has an academic center, with a performing arts department that in recent years has gained visibility and esteem throughout the academic community. As an added bonus, the Tilden Arts Center at Cape Cod Community College, built in 1976, produces a full slate of productions open to the community, with some presented in its expansive, seven-hundred-seat theater, and others in the more diminutive studio, which seats just two hundred. And, when students aren't using the stages to showcase their work, locals can use the state-of-the-art facilities for school graduations, town hall meetings or dance recitals.

According to the school's website (www.capecod.edu/web/tilden), the center was built as part of an expansion to the college campus.

> In 1991, it was named for W. Culver Tilden, who retired from a career in taxidermy in Palmyra, NY to Eastham, MA, with his wife Gretchen. According to records, Tilden was a gentle and private man who was often seen on campus in a bright red sport coat and Scottish plaid cap. Over the years, the venue has served as a cultural hub for the arts with a long and respected history of presenting and producing artistic works by local, regional and international artists.

But Vana Trudeau, Tilden Arts Center coordinator, says that the center's primary raison d'être is to educate through performance. "Everything we do is aimed at providing a complete educational experience; we exist to create a learning lab for our students. In fact, we see ourselves as an incubator not only for performance artists, but also for stage managers and techs," she says. "In fact, if you look at theaters around the Cape, it's likely that their techs and stage managers have come from here. We feed the whole theater system."

To create that "complete educational experience," Trudeau and her staff often work with teachers to coordinate curricula, for instance pairing assignments in English literature classes with productions. And, while that could mean reading and performing in a show like *Macbeth*, it could also mean exposure to new and experimental works.

"We want students to be exposed to all kinds of roles. That often means being exposed to new and experimental works. They need to know how to handle these kinds of roles, as well as Shakespeare," she says. "There's no reason that one should preclude the other."

As examples of some of the experimental works the center has done, in October 2018, Trudeau directed *Dead Man's Cell Phone*, an imaginative comedy by MacArthur Genius Grant recipient and Pulitzer Prize finalist Sarah Ruhl. Then, in the spring of 2019, the department offered *The Curious Incident of the Dog in the Night-Time*, Simon Stephens's adaptation of the acclaimed Mark Haddon novel, and winner of the 2015 Tony Award for Best Play.

In fact, the center reserves its fall performance slots for shows that provide exposure to either classics or new and important works. For example, the fall 2016 show was Shakespeare's *Twelfth Night*, while the next year's offering was *Too Much Light Makes the Baby Go Blind*, an ensemble experiment in presenting "30 Plays in 60 Minutes." Each two-minute play is performed in random order with an interactive audience. An onstage sixty-minute timer keeps everyone honest. In the spring semester, the center works to "engage the community" with plays that have social relevance, says Trudeau. For example, in the spring of 2017, the choice was *1984*, with *Urinetown*, which deals with conservation, chosen for the spring 2018 semester.

Whatever the production, Trudeau says it offers a chance for students "to get their hands dirty," actually working on the show. That hands-on experience has proven invaluable to students who have gone on to careers in television and regional theaters. And even if a student never pursues an acting career, living through the experience of climbing on a stage and speaking lines leads to growth, Trudeau says. "When a student takes a theater class, they learn to look someone in the eye and talk to them. It's an incredible confidence builder."

Shakespeare and Seminars

In the summer of 2018, the center took to the road for its inaugural season of Shakespeare Under the Stars. A blended group of students and community actors performed in a seventy-five-minute version of *The Tempest* on the Hyannis Village Green, the Salt Pond Visitor Center at the Cape Cod National Seashore in Eastham and at Mashpee Commons' new outdoor stage. Directed by Eric Joseph, executive director of the Bay Colony Shakespeare Company, the production was presented on various Mondays and Fridays in July and August.

According to Trudeau, "the response was so great, we'll be doing more in the years to come. It's amazing what happens when you get Shakespeare out in the air; people really respond to it!"

And, in 2013, '14 and '15, the college played host to the Kennedy Center American College Regional Theatre Festival and will again in 2019, '20 and '21. The festival involves 1,500 students from fifty schools and features five days of workshops/seminars, conferences, performances and speeches by noted playwrights. Trudeau, currently serving as co–vice chair of the regional event, will take on the co-chairposition for the region beginning in 2021 and continuing through 2023. "It's a fabulous event, and it brings in more than $1 million to the region in January—a time when the Cape really needs the income," Trudeau says.

The center's website sums up its contribution to the Cape community with the following: "With two performance spaces, two functional art studios, music practice rooms and the Higgins Art Gallery, we serve the community year-round with activities and programming for all ages."

Over the past forty years, the Tilden Arts Center has hosted Opera New England, Art Garfunkel, comedian Bob Marley, the Edwards Twins Impersonators and Up With People, and it has produced works ranging from Shakespeare to Durang and from Vonnegut to Albee. The staged reading series, Play with Your Food, presents new works by local and regional playwrights.

Clearly, the theaters at the center of Cape Cod have, through the years, been at the heart of the theater world on the peninsula. But it's also clear that, like the beautiful landscape and seascape, the power of theater doesn't diminish as you move toward the mainland. The towns around the bridges are also awash in theater history, with a range of fascinating connections to the theater world both on-Cape and off. We continue our story with that history.

6

THEATER IN THE UPPER CAPE

NEAR THE MAINLAND BUT WORLDS AWAY

W hen you think of Falmouth, streets of graceful old homes and village greens come to mind. And Woods Hole is of course associated with the oceanographic institute that bears its name. But the area also has a distinguished theater history, with some groups still mounting productions and others that have unfortunately faded into memory. Here is a look at that history.

THE UNIVERSITY PLAYERS OF CAPE COD

The history of the University Players of Cape Cod actually goes back to the 1920s (so, almost to the very beginnings of theater on Cape Cod), when a troupe of actors—whose members were students of Harvard, Princeton and Radcliffe, hence the name—began performing in the area.

One of the young and "starving" artists in the group was Joshua Logan, who would go on to an incredibly successful career on Broadway and in Hollywood. During his last year at Princeton, Logan earned a scholarship that allowed him to study acting under theater guru Konstantin Stanislavsky in Moscow. He made his Broadway debut as an actor in 1932 and soon began working as an assistant stage manager and then as a director. His Hollywood career began in the mid-1930s, when he worked as a dialogue director on a pair of films starring Charles Boyer. Then, in 1938, Logan and Arthur Ripley codirected Henry Fonda in *I Met My Love Again*. He then went

University Players production of *The Jazz Age*, circa 1930. *Courtesy Falmouth Museums on the Green.*

on to direct plays and films from the 1940s through the 1960s, including such classics as *Annie Get Your Gun* on Broadway and the film *Bus Stop* with Marilyn Monroe.

But it all began on Cape Cod for Logan and a number of other soon-to-be-greats, including Henry Fonda, Jimmy Stewart, stage and screen star Margaret Sullavan, future *Life* photographer John Swope, character actress Mildred Natwick, Arlene Francis and Martin Gabel. (Think about it; like so many seemingly inconsequential groups on Cape Cod, the Players had an enormous influence on the entertainment world. It was the nest that nurtured Joshua Logan, Henry Fonda and Jimmy Stewart!)

In his autobiography, *My Up and Down, In and Out Life*, Logan wrote about the "starving artist" summers he spent in West Falmouth:

> *Inside each member burned hot love not only for the theatre but for their company—yes, and for each other. We actually believed we were better than anyone. We would have challenged any company in the country. It was only this blind, idiot confidence that could make us accept minor parts, odd jobs with the crew, our meager salary of five dollars a week less laundry, our frayed clothing and our repetitious skimpy diet.*

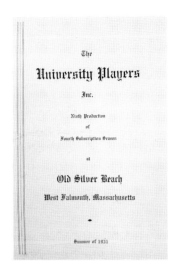

The
University Players
Inc.

Ninth Production
of
Fourth Subscription Season

at

Old Silver Beach

West Falmouth, Massachusetts

•

Summer of 1931

University Players vintage program, 1931. *Courtesy Falmouth Museums on the Green.*

In the beginning, in the mid-1920s, the troupe used various spaces around the area for rehearsals, performances and lodging. One home in Woods Hole—part of the historic Whitecrest estate, owned by Frances Crane—served as rehearsal space at the time. (Unfortunately, the old building was recently lost to a fire.) There was separate housing for the actors and actresses, with the young women staying in a chaperoned house and the actors sometimes using troupe member Charles Leatherbee's grandfather's yacht as their dormitory. Eventually, the troupe took over a block in Old Silver Beach that had once housed bathhouses and a hot dog stand to serve as rehearsal and performance space. The actors were housed in West Falmouth.

Sadly, the group disbanded after just a few years—one of the casualties of the Great Depression. But, like so many groups on the Cape, it was an incubator for talent, with some of its members going on to stunning careers on Broadway and in Hollywood.

In his autobiography, *Fonda—My Life*, alum Henry Fonda notes that he once said, "The only people who've seen me are visitors to Cape Cod." Thanks to his apprenticeship in Falmouth, that statement soon seemed the height of irony.

THE FALMOUTH PLAYHOUSE: THE JEWEL IN THE CROWN

The town of Falmouth is noted for its physical beauty and attention to the arts, so it's probably no surprise that the once-spectacular Falmouth Playhouse has often been called the most beautiful summer playhouse in the country. In fact, in her book *Theater on Cape Cod*, Evelyn Lawson titles her chapter on the playhouse "The Most Beautiful Summer Theater."

And here's how she describes the site of the Playhouse: "It is located in an unspoiled, woodland setting, overlooking a small, clear lake. And the building was positioned to be reflected in its shimmering waters. Terraces of interesting stonework were built on the lakeside, a complement to the rural beauty."

Unfortunately, the Playhouse no longer stands. On February 28, 1994, following a period of financial difficulties for then-owner Ralph Miller, the building burned to the ground. Sound suspicious? Miller's insurance company thought so too. It seemed especially dicey because Miller had already collected large sums from at least two other suspicious fires and a bankruptcy. (Subsequently, in 2009, his Pocono Playhouse also burned to the ground.) The company filed suit against him, but arson was never proven, so the once-beautiful testament to the beauty of theater was gone for good. But the long history of the building—before and after it became a gathering place for the stars—remains.

As Lawson wrote, the building once stood on a beautiful wooded lot in the Hatchville section of Falmouth, on the shore of Coonamessett Pond. Before becoming a theater, it had been part of a 350-acre farm. The farm was the brainchild of Concord farmer and state agriculturalist Wilfrid Wheeler, who talked industrialist Charles Crane into helping to bankroll the operation. (Remember the Crane name from the section on the University Players? The name turns up again and again in the business and theatrical history of Falmouth.) The huge operation yielded a number of products, including milk, poultry and eggs and a variety of crops. In time, the farm had twelve houses and twenty-five farm buildings. Eventually, the site was developed into a resort with a renovated farmhouse called the Coonamessett Inn, which was soon enlarged. By 1933, the Coonamessett Resort had an eighteen-hole golf course, an airport, tennis courts, a polo field and beach cabanas.

I told you all of that so I could tell you this: After Charles Crane died in 1939, his two children managed the resort, which boasted twenty-five rental cottages and a barnlike indoor recreation center called the Coonamessett Club. This structure, when remodeled and air-conditioned, became the 650-seat Falmouth Playhouse. (An interesting note about the theater's cooling system: It was initially equipped with just a system of fans that brought in cool air and circulated it through vents under the seats. Then, in 1956, modern air-conditioning was added. Air-conditioning—or the lack thereof—is a big deal in the theater world. Remember that theatergoers originally made their way to Cape Cod's venues to escape the stifling little boxes on Broadway.)

The playhouse was the jewel in the crown of Richard Aldrich, who, as we discussed in the previous chapter, was largely responsible for the stunning success of the Cape Playhouse in Dennis and eventually added the Melody Tent and South Shore Music Circus, along with the Falmouth venue, to his theater empire, signing a long-term lease with the Cranes.

Vintage picture of Falmouth Playhouse. *Courtesy Falmouth Museums on the Green.*

Aldrich supervised the renovations, which resulted in the fabulous structure Lawson describes this way in her book:

> *Since the playhouse was in "real country" distant from dining facilities, an extension for a glassed-in dining area overlooking the lake was added to the structure. After the fashion of the English theaters, an extensive oval bar was included in the lobby....Even an area between the dining room and lobby bar was arranged for nightclub, after-show entertainment.*

Aldrich was determined to fuel his Falmouth operation with the same kind of star power that had proven successful in Dennis—and would inevitably fuel all of his enterprises. More than just professional actors, he wanted names that rang bells with the theatergoing public. A look at some of the casts from the first few seasons tells the story. Cast members included Tallulah Bankhead, Helen Hayes, Gertrude Lawrence (Aldrich's wife), Joan Blondell, Lillian Gish, Paulette Goddard, John Garfield, Veronica Lake, Hume Cronyn, Dana Andrews, Walter Matthau and Eva Gabor.

(Here's a cool piece of trivia: The theater was christened when Bankhead smashed a champagne bottle against a stage prop.)

Aldrich operated the theater for four seasons before determining that he was spread too thin with multiple venues. He sold out to Sidney Gordon, a Boston-area theater lover who continued to adhere to Aldrich's star system. In the first few years of her tenure—which turned out to span twenty-five years—she brought back Hayes and Bankhead and added such stars as Edward Everett Horton, Carol Channing and—rather spectacularly—Marlon Brando. During the Gordon years, a number of shows were staged in Falmouth before eventually becoming big Broadway hits. One example was *Dear Charles*, with Bankhead, which went on to become the big hit of the 1954 season in New York. (Here's an interesting tidbit: Gordon brought in a production of *Autumn Crocus*, featuring President Harry Truman's daughter, Margaret.)

Playbills and posters in the archives of the Falmouth Museums on the Green offer some clues about the timing of some shows during the Gordon era. Although information about production dates is a little thin, here's an entry the museum posted on its website (www.museumsonthegreen.org):

> *Our playbills undoubtedly date from Gordon's era, but deducing exact dates is tricky, since no years are inscribed. Entering play titles into a search of the Enterprise online archive (which only goes up to 1962), yielded one result—a Myrna Loy vehicle called* There Must Be a Pony, *staged in 1962. The Loy poster lists the theater's phone number as LO3-5922, while other posters use the newer, all-numeric form 563-5922, indicating a post-1962 production date. One poster teases an upcoming run of the musical* Godspell, *thereby placing its time frame post-1971. Another promotes Alan Sues, a regular on TV's* Laugh-In, *indicating a date of 1968 or later.*
>
> *The playbill featuring Academy Award winner Joan Fontaine (*Suspicion, *1940) particularly caught our eye. As part of our ongoing effort to digitize late 20th century slides and negatives in our collection, we had recently scanned some slides, labeled 1970, which showed Fontaine enjoying a clambake in Falmouth. We wondered if the clambake coincided with her run in* Relatively Speaking.

(The museum historians go on to share this little tidbit: One of the added little treats about the Cape theater world in its heyday is that fans often encountered big stars like Fontaine at a clambake, on the beach or in the shops. For example, Julie Harris, who was a presence in so many theaters on the Cape, was an inveterate shopper; fans talk about seeing her in shops around Chatham and the Lower Cape.)

Ralph Miller (I can hardly resist calling him Nero, for "fiddling" when the Playhouse burned) purchased the theater in 1984 for what then

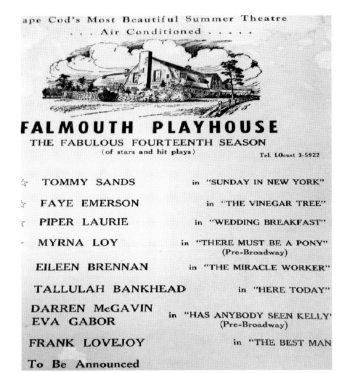

Right: Vintage
Falmouth Playhouse
poster. *Courtesy
Falmouth Museums on
the Green.*

Below: Falmouth
Playhouse programs.
*Courtesy Falmouth
Museums on the Green.*

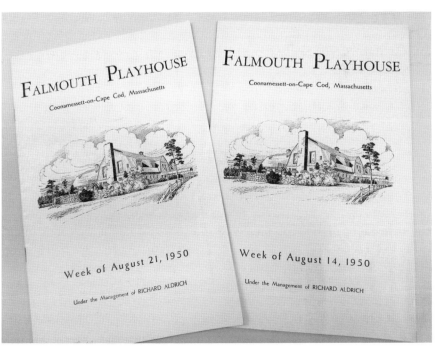

seemed like the massive sum of $420,000. Almost immediately—and true to form, considering his business history—he mired the theater in financial difficulties. Of course, this was a time when theaters began to suffer under the growing weight of royalties, Actors' Equity fees and the cost of maintaining a resident company—coupled with the impact of television. But it's hard not to think that there wasn't more than a touch of mismanagement involved in the decline and demise ten years later of the once-spectacular Falmouth Playhouse.

Fortunately, the theater culture continues to thrive and grow on Cape Cod. But it's hard not to mourn the loss of a virtual institution like the Falmouth Playhouse, once a symbol of the golden age of theater.

College Light Opera Company: The Cape's Theater Boot Camp

When you drive up to the Highfield Theatre in Falmouth, where both the College Light Opera Company (CLOC) and Falmouth Theatre Guild perform, the feeling is one of absolute majesty. The theater is situated atop a hill, and to reach it you wind through a lush, green landscape, with Highfield Hall its graceful, Victorian centerpiece. It seems uniquely appropriate that these groups, each with a long and distinguished history, should call the historic theater their performance home.

The theater, built in 1876, is at the apex of an estate nestled in the Beebe Woods section of Falmouth. On its website (www.collegelightoperacompany.com), CLOC outlines the early history of the theater, which eventually became the group's summer home.

Before this classic summer stock theatre opened its doors to audiences in 1947, it housed a very different patronage. Originally built as a barn and stables, historic Highfield Theatre was an out building of Highfield Hall, providing the homes for Pierson Beebe's prized horses, Salaam and Ali Baba. In 1947, Arthur Beckhard purchased Highfield Hall, Barn and Tanglewood Estate along with 200 acres of beautiful Beebe Woods with the intention of housing a summer theater, originally conceived as Tanglewood Theatre.

Beckhard, producer of the biggest hit of the 1932 spring season on Broadway, *Another Language*, had been a supporter of Falmouth's University

Players early on. But it appears Beckhard wasn't much of a businessman, because the original Tanglewood Theatre lasted only two seasons. Luckily—for Beckhard and the Cape Cod theater world—just when the wolves were at the door, a savior was at hand. Local philanthropist DeWitt Ter Heun bought Beckhard's mortgage and kept him on to direct the policies and theater production.

The new team started the 1949 season on top of the world in their hilltop theater, but disaster was about to strike. That was the season that Richard Aldrich opened the Falmouth Playhouse just a few miles away, earning a steady flow of rave reviews. (When Tallulah Bankhead christened the Playhouse with champagne, it marked the end of Tanglewood.) Despite lofty goals, Beckhard was unable to compete with Aldrich and his deep theater experience and bottomless pockets. Enter Kingsley Perry, one of the founders of the University Players, who (not surprisingly) set up a company of young college students. While Perry left before the end of the first season, the theater was left in the hands of assistant director Richard Maxson, who laid the groundwork for a successful theater in Falmouth. It was during the next few years that the theater really became a part of the Falmouth theater scene.

By 1954, Ter Heun had had enough of the theater world and gave control of the theater over to a group that sourced talent largely from Williams College and a number of other women's colleges in the area. They named the new company Cross Right Stage. The group lasted a few years and had one particularly notable moment.

In his 1995 article "Curtain Rising: Theater in Falmouth over the Past Seventy Years" in *Spritsail* magazine, DeWitt C. Jones III recounts the event. "On the evening of August 31, 1954, just after Hurricane Carol hit Cape Cod, Cross Right Stage had the distinction of being the only theater that had a show. Fifty-five people watched *Mr. Roberts* by candlelight. George Oppenheimer, noted playwright, called it 'one of the most exciting evenings I have ever spent in theatre.'"

During the Cross Right era, there was something else going on in town. A group from Oberlin College in Ohio was performing Gilbert and Sullivan operettas, first at the Mashpee town hall, then at the local high school. By the time Cross Right had run its course, Oberlin was ready to take up residence in the theater atop the hill. Beginning in 1958, the troupe became permanent summer residents at Highfield Theatre, presenting an annual menu of Gilbert and Sullivan and other American and European operettas. The Oberlin company spent summers at Highfield Theatre before moving

Left: Cross Right Stage program. *Courtesy Falmouth Museums on the Green.*

Right: Oberlin College/Gilbert & Sullivan Players poster for *The Mikado. Courtesy Falmouth Museums on the Green.*

operations back to Ohio in 1968. On its website, CLOC notes the key role Oberlin played in laying the groundwork for its own company. "It is to their credit that the Highfield Theatre summer light opera and musical theatre tradition was established. Audiences were dazzled by a fine-voiced vocal company, a live 30+ orchestra and fully produced shows with costumes, scenery and sets."

MORPHING INTO CLOC

So the groundwork was set, and two members of the Oberlin group decided to take advantage of that fact. Donald Tull and Robert Haslun joined forces to found a new company, the College Light Opera Company, based on the Oberlin G&S players. Besides the burgeoning reputation of the theater, the pair inherited a few helpful accoutrements. According to the CLOC site, "Securing various costumes, props, furniture and a list of 1968 Oberlin G&S patrons, the two founders embarked upon a wild and tumultuous journey to bring light opera and musical theater back to Highfield Theatre."

But the pair was also determined to make a number of adjustments designed to spur financial success and bring the group a little more into the modern era. For starters, they expanded the season from eight to nine weeks, cut the size of the company in half and replaced the orchestra with two piano players. And, in keeping with the group's new name, CLOC varied its repertoire, making room for some more contemporary musical works. That was a move designed to bolster the box office but also to vary the experience for company members. That first season, the company still featured five G&S operettas (*Trial by Jury*, *The Pirates of Penzance*, *Iolanthe*, *The Mikado* and *Princess Ida*). But the new managers added *The Beggar's Opera*, *Die Fledermaus* and the Broadway sensations *Brigadoon* and *The Fantasticks*.

Mark Pearson, the company's current producer and artistic director, notes that a wider variety of offerings is a benefit for potential company members. "It's a huge plus to have CLOC on your resume. It says that you've had wide-ranging experience." These days, he says, the group works on a system of threes: three operettas, three contemporary/golden age musicals and three "wild cards." For example, in the 2018 season, two of the wild cards were the slightly offbeat musicals *Pippin* and *Sweeney Todd*. And there's another criterion for a season's choices. Pearson says: "We always try to bring in at least one unusual show that the cast wouldn't have a chance to do anywhere else. That's where the educational part of what we do comes in."

From the start, all company members were hired on an equal footing, with auditions for even lead roles open to all members, Pearson says. He adds that the company endeavors to bring on performers with a range of voice types (for example, tenor, soprano, etcetera), with particular emphasis on vocalists who can "cross over from one type to another." And he adds that vocalists perform in every production during a season, emphasizing that this is "part of the educational aspect of CLOC."

Unfortunately, the first summer season (1969) was a bit of a financial disappointment. (Ticket prices for that season ranged from $2.75 to $3.75, which seems inconceivable now.) So the next year, the group doubled the size of the company and brought back an orchestra. That seemed to give the group the leverage it needed to boost ticket sales and bring in more subscribers. By the end of the season, the books balanced—by what in today's standards would be a miniscule amount, but anything in black is obviously better than bleeding red all over a balance sheet. And the return to a larger company and well-populated orchestra pit afforded a feeling of

College Light Opera Company production of *Princess Ida*, 1972. *Courtesy CLOC staff.*

substance and musicality. (To this day, it's impressive when the full orchestra at CLOC productions tunes up and the full company fills the stage.)

(When Tull moved on to other ventures in 1973, Haslun continued as CLOC's sole producer, with Ursula Rooth, Haslun's colleague from the 1969 inaugural company, continuing as business manager. Then, in June, before the 1975 season opened, Haslun and Rooth were married. The pair continued to manage the company until turning over the reins to Pearson and producer and executive E. Mark Murphy in 2015.)

In the first years of the new company, the resident cast and crew were housed in the nearby Tanglewood Estate, which was convenient but, unfortunately, not very spacious. According to Jones in his *Spiritsail* article, "The entire company was housed in Tanglewood [a sister estate to Highfield Hall], which also included a rehearsal hall and dining room. It was such a tight squeeze that on pleasant days many of the company ate outdoors. When it rained, the congestion indoors made for very fast meals."

Just a few years later, in 1974, the owners of Tanglewood decided to tear down the hall that had housed CLOC throughout their summer seasons. But, as is often the case in Falmouth—and in the theater world in general—generous philanthropists rose to the occasion. In this case, it was Josiah and Josephine Lilly who made space available to the group in the form of an estate that had been the West Falmouth Inn. Built in 1895 for Sara M. Skull of Philadelphia, it was initially called Bridgefields Hall because it stood beside the bridge to Chapoquoit Island. The estate was purchased in 1911 by Katherine A. Montgomery, who established the West Falmouth Inn in 1912, with its popular Popponessett West restaurant.

CLOC moved to the West Falmouth campus in 1975 and purchased the six-acre property from the Lillys in 1979. The living quarters and rehearsal spaces have remained there ever since.

Over the years, additions to the estate have included twin cottages on the harbor, a caretaker's cottage and a staff cottage. (You may be getting the feeling at this stage that the town of Falmouth is a little piece of heaven filled with green and gracious estates—and you'd be right!) To this day, the full company of about eighty-five is housed at the estate. For the most recent, 2018, season, the company included thirty-two vocalists, eighteen orchestral musicians, twelve scenic and costume technicians, three designers, two collaborative pianists, two associate conductors, one choreographer, one stage manager and four administrators. And applicants who make the cut—about 26 percent for the most recent season—are afforded room and board for their eleven-week stay, with stipends provided to orchestra members. (Pearson notes that one of the drawing cards for applicants is the chance to work with the ultra-talented technicians, choreographers, stage managers and set and costume designers. "When we're putting together a production, we see it all as a work of art—from set design, to choreography to performance.")

In describing life at the West Falmouth estate, Caroline Lloyd, CLOC trustee and former board president of the Falmouth Historical Society, noted the following in her article "Celebrating 50 Years of the College Light Opera Company," published as part of the Falmouth Historical Society's exhibit of the same name.

Performing six times a week, students rehearse during the day at the Inn at West Falmouth for the upcoming week's new production. At any given time, a staging rehearsal could be happening in the living room, a choral rehearsal in the dining room, a choreography run-through out on the lawn, coaching in the cottages, small groups working on the deck, and other preparations taking place virtually anywhere else space can be found. All the while costumes are being sewn in a back room and sets are being built behind the theater.

On its website, CLOC notes that the 1980s and 1990s saw a huge increase in its repertoire, applications and patronage. That gave the group room to grow. According to the history, "While the 1970s had been a decade of establishing the company's reputation and membership, the next two would carve out the company's sound, vision and mission. Productions from that

College Light Opera Company production of *HMS Pinafore*, cast picture, *1983. CLOC staff.*

era included *The Dollar Princess* (Fall), *Plain and Fancy*, *Man of La Mancha*, *George M!*, *West Side Story*, *Robert and Elizabeth*, *Fiddler on the Roof*, and the smash hit *A Funny Thing Happened on the Way to the Forum.*"

Moving into the next century, the group has continued to offer premieres while also, according to its history, "reviving classic musicals and breathing new life into European and American operetta." One sterling production was the 2008 premiere of a new rendering of Jerome Kern's 1927 classic *Show Boat*, starring Ryan Speedo Green as Joe and Dominique Sharpton (daughter of the Reverend Al Sharpton) as Queenie.

A June 16, 2019 CBS News article said this about Green: "The high priest in the temple of the Metropolitan Opera in New York is Ryan Speedo Green, starring in Rossini's *Semiramide*. Green blessed the hall with a voice that reaches from bass to baritone. At age 32, he is a member of the Vienna State Opera and performs on stages of the world in German, French, English and Italian."

In 2018, as the theater turned fifty, it stood as the largest summer resident company in the United States. That of course means that students from all over the country—and the world—will continue to vie for the right to step foot on the Highfield stage. To date, the theater counts 3,500 alumni.

As Lloyd notes in her article, "CLOC cultivates the next generation of professionals who will shape American theater through their professional work on- and off-stage in theaters, universities, cultural organizations, and non-profits."

F. Paul Driscoll, editor-in-chief of *Opera News* and CLOC alumnus, is quoted in Lloyd's article: "Since its inaugural season, CLOC still remains true to its purpose: to provide young and still-developing artists with an atmosphere where they can learn their craft, challenge their skills, and celebrate their talents. It engages these young artists in the business of presenting quality living theater."

Falmouth Theatre Guild: Sixty Years and Counting

It was in 1957 that the Falmouth Theatre Guild came together, and from the beginning, it was a community theater dedicated to longevity. "We now have three generations in the theater, with young people coming in all the time," says longtime member Matthew Gould, who first joined the group in 1978. "It's really like one big family; I've made all of my best friends in the theater," he said in an interview with me.

Gould talks on a break from constructing the set for the group's next production at Falmouth's Highfield Theatre, where rows of lighting equipment hang in the ancient rafters. The Guild is the winter occupant of the site, with CLOC taking over in the summer months, as noted earlier in this chapter. But early on—like so many groups in their infancy—the Guild mounted productions in found spaces around town. (The very first show the group mounted was *Goodbye My Fancy*, which had been a Broadway hit ten years before. The show is a sophisticated comedy that spins the tale of a congresswoman who finds love at her old alma mater. Joan Crawford stars in the 1951 film version.)

In the early 1960s, one of the group's founding members, Kitty Baker, negotiated a deal with the Highfield Theatre's then-owner, DeWitt Ter Heun, to establish the group as the theater's off-season residents. That meant no more carting lighting and staging equipment back and forth for productions, Gould says, especially because CLOC and the Guild now share a great deal of the expensive and unwieldy equipment. And, luckily for the group, the arrangement has held through the years, with the Cape Cod Conservatory—the current owners of the building and grounds—now the landlords.

Of course, no arrangement is ever perfect, and over the years the group has had to undertake a number of projects to modernize and winterize the building, taking a bite out of its bank account. Still, the Guild is uniquely successful for a community theater, thanks in part to what longtime member (since the 1960s) and group historian Gil Rapoza calls "an incredibly efficient ticketing operation." In fact, the group is so financially stable that every year it is able to dole out thousands of dollars in scholarships to students pursuing careers in theater and the arts.

Both Rapoza and Gould also credit the shows that make it to the theater marquee every fall, winter and spring for the health of the group's coffers; generally speaking, the group has relied on a menu of comedies and musicals to bring in the crowds. Over the years, shows have included *The King and I*, *My Fair Lady*, *The Music Man*, *South Pacific*, *Anything Goes*, *Chicago*, *Young Frankenstein* and *A Christmas Carol*. Recently, the Guild mounted a production of *Peter Pan*, with newly installed equipment allowing them to send characters soaring across the stage.

The group is also fortunate, Gould and Rapoza say, to be based in a community with a long history of support for the arts and to be close to both Woods Hole and Boston, with their active and well-educated young

Falmouth Theatre Guild, *A Christmas Carol*, 2015. *Falmouth Theatre Guild staff.*

professionals. "So many theater companies have only older members, making it hard to keep operating into the future. We're lucky that is not the case for us," Rapoza says.

One final note: There are wonderful stories about another resident of the theater, a spirit of a young woman who stage crew members swear sometimes shows up to supervise late-night set construction. And—like most members of the theater community—she seems to crave attention. One night, she appeared to push down seatbacks along a whole row of seating.

Just one more temperamental leading lady!

THE CAPE COD THEATRE PROJECT

Another group in the Falmouth area—this one relatively new—has also benefitted from the arts- and theater-friendly atmosphere on the Cape. Back in the mid-1990s, two actors who had been longtime summer visitors to the peninsula decided to take advantage of what they saw as "the perfect sanctuary for developing new work, combining an idyllic and comforting atmosphere with a community that enjoys and engages with the arts." That's how the Cape Cod Theatre Project's online history (www.capecodtheatreproject.org) describes the decision by Andrew Polk and Jim Bracchitta to bring new works to the Cape, allowing fledgling playwrights to get their sea legs (if you'll excuse the pun).

The group began by mounting productions at the Woods Hole Community Center every July. Now, the Project brings in four plays a year, mounting a new production for each of the four weeks in July. And the group has a more permanent summer locale, the beautiful Falmouth Academy. The company brings in a new cast of professional (Equity) actors every Sunday, followed by twenty-nine hours of rehearsals over the next few days and performances mounted as staged readings Thursday through Saturday. Performances are followed by feedback sessions with audiences. It's a rigorous boot camp for new playwrights, actors and directors

This gives playwrights a chance to get real-life reactions to work, often prompting revisions before they take their plays back to New York or other major markets, says Hal Brooks, current artistic director. "It's all about incubation for new plays."

And this "incubation period" has proven incredibly effective, with forty-six of the sixty-eight productions having gone on to successful runs either on Broadway, Off-Broadway or at regional theaters around the world. One recent example is Mike Daisey's celebrated run of *The Agony and the Ecstasy of Steve Jobs* at the Public Theater. Another is *Hillary and Clinton*, which recently opened at Broadway's Golden Theatre. According to a March 16, 2019 edition of *Playbill*, "Two-time Tony Award, and three-time Emmy winner Laurie Metcalf, and two-time Tony Award and six-time Emmy winner John Lithgow return to Broadway to star in *Hillary and Clinton*, a new play by Tony nominee Lucas Hnath (*A Doll's House, Part 2*)."

Other venues include Manhattan Theater Club, Playwrights Horizons, the Roundabout Theater, the Daryl Roth Theater, Rattlestick Theater, Berkeley Repertory Theater, the La Jolla Playhouse, the Repertory Theater of St. Louis, Dallas Theater Center and the Magic Theater.

One problem the group faces every summer is finding space to house its casts and crews. "Real estate is always a challenge in summer on Cape Cod. Let's hope we can continue to find space for our people every year so we can continue to foster new ideas," Brooks says.

Woods Hole: Where Science and Art Come Together

When you think of the harbor-side town of Woods Hole, the oceanographic institute that bears its name immediately comes to mind. But, besides being home to some of the greatest scientific minds in the world, the community has its artistic side; it is home to a theater company that has actually been around since 1975. The Woods Hole Theater Company (WHTC), which began life as the Woods Hole Theatre Festival, was originally the brainchild of a group of young professionals from New York that actually performed in space in lab buildings, mounting as many as twelve productions a year.

According to Joan Edstrom, longtime WHTC board member and inveterate theater director, in those early years, the company was in fact fueled by a steady influx of young people—often graduates of dramatic arts programs—coming to the Cape to pay the rent with service-related jobs. "Their service jobs weren't too demanding, so they had free time to dedicate to the theater," she says.

The group grew through the 1970s and '80s, with a special summer show added to the off-season production calendar. "At one point we would bring in a director from New York for a show, and a contributor would pay for them and put them up," Edstrom says.

These days the company is all-volunteer. As members of other companies have noted, this can put a troupe at a disadvantage. "If you have a huge

Right: WHTC production of *Vanya & Sonia & Masha & Spike*. WHTC staff.

Below: WHTC production of *Come Back to the Five & Dime, Jimmy Dean*. WHTC staff.

budget and are paying nine staff people, there's so much you can do. If you're all-volunteer, it's a little harder to compete with all the theater companies around," Edstrom says.

And, as time has gone by, the company—like so many other community theaters—has found it harder to recruit young members. "These days, so many young people have demanding careers. That makes it difficult for them to dedicate time to a theater group like ours," Edstrom says. She adds, however, that—in typical Cape theater style—the company often "borrows" cast and crew from groups around the Cape.

On a positive note, the company now has a permanent home in the Woods Hole Community Center, which sits right on the town's picturesque harbor. One more of Cape Cod's historic structures, it was built in 1878 and is part of a group of historic buildings maintained by the Woods Hole Community Association. While the available space is nothing if not modest, it is a casual, intimate setting that brings the audience up close and personal to the action on the small stage. That makes it perfectly suited to the children's shows that are now liberally sprinkled through the group's production schedule.

For example, during a recent production of *The Terrible Infants*, the audience of adults and youngsters is drawn into the fantasy world onstage. As *Miro* magazine wrote about the show, which originated on the London stage: "*The Terrible Infants* is unashamedly fantastical. It takes the form of a series of macabre stories, which all play out in a Tim Burton–esque world. The show captures one of the things I like best about the theatre: a youthful glee at watching a production that conjures entire worlds out of everyday odd objects."

But the group is hardly limited to children's theater. For instance, 2019 productions included *Weekend Comedy*, a light look at what happens when two couples book the same weekend cottage, and *Mia's Cloud*, a futuristic look at the impact of artificial intelligence on a normal family, written by local playwright Gary Vacon.

Unfortunately, while the center offers available space for all WHTC productions, it is also available to other groups, meaning that the all-volunteer WHTC isn't able to completely give up its wandering ways. "When we have productions we have to cart equipment back-and-forth, which isn't always easy," Edstrom says.

Still, after almost five decades performing at harbor-side, it seems likely the group will continue to live up to its tagline, "Inspiring audiences with the magic of the arts."

Cotuit Center for the Arts: Educate, Entertain, Illuminate, Inspire

For the twenty-plus years of its life, the Cotuit Center for the Arts has been on a mission, but not just to entertain. It seeks to "Educate, Entertain, Illuminate, Inspire." Those are the words the center uses to lead into its mission statement, which goes on to read: "The arts are essential. Our mission is to be a welcoming hub for Cape Cod's artists, performers, students, and audiences, working together to make the creation and experience of art accessible, nurturing, and thrilling to all."

Perhaps the most descriptive phrase is "welcoming hub." Situated in Cotuit, one of the seven villages of Barnstable, the center sits on a two-acre expanse of land on Route 28, one of the main highways of Cape Cod. It's a place where you can take an art class, see a gallery exhibit, watch a film and—just incidentally—see a live theater production or two (one in the center's 175-seat main stage and another in the diminutive Black Box Theater), all in the same day. This stands as perhaps the clearest illustration in the area of "becoming all thing to all people" as a way to thrive in a market rife with competition. In fact, on average, the center hosts more than thirty-five thousand visitors yearly.

According to the center's site (www.artsonthecape.org):

> *A typical week at the center juggles an average of 120 hours of programming across ten schedulable locations on campus. From rehearsals to meetings to classes to performances, we are always buzzing with activity. A typical year will feature eight Mainstage theater productions, eleven Black Box shows, forty or so class offerings, twelve gallery installations, and forty special events from concerts to student collaborations, annual festivals to talent showcases, craft fairs to magic shows.*

In a deceptively inauspicious beginning, the center was established in 1993 in a 1,200-square-foot former mechanic's garage, where founders began by offering art classes and exhibition space. Then, in 1996, the group staged its first theatrical productions, proving from the start that the company wouldn't shy away from a challenge. That first season included productions of *Hamlet*; *Macbeth*; Sam Shepard's *Fool for Love*; *The Gift of the Gorgon*, which explores the themes of forgiveness and revenge; and *Terra Nova*, a play about survival set in Antarctica.

"We look for the highest quality in everything we do, from the quality of the art in our gallery to the quality of productions," explains David Kuehn, executive director of the center. "When it comes to productions, we're not afraid to tackle something edgy. It's okay to do *Annie*, but we also have a responsibility to deal with controversial issues."

In April 2000, the garage burned to the ground. Ironically enough, this turned out to be the impetus for development into a comprehensive center capable of bringing the "thrill of the arts" to large groups of people. By the fall of that year, the group had found its current, two-acre site on Route 28, which included two buildings that could immediately be put to use for classes, exhibitions and small-scale theater productions, with some productions also staged at Cotuit's Freedom Hall.

It was clear the Cotuit community had been awaiting just the kind of comprehensive arts hub the center represented. "From the very beginning, we worked hard to engage the community in everything we did, and it has really paid off. We realize we have to constantly reach out beyond four walls to keep the community engaged," Kuehn says. "We want to create a culture of inclusion; when people walk through the door we want them to feel they belong."

Kuehn's sentiment is echoed in the group's mission statement: "We collaborate with local artists, musicians, actors, performers, teachers, volunteers, and the occasional celebrity to provide a rich experience to our audiences and attendees all year long."

In one case, the center moved out beyond the borders of the village, creating a four-way partnership with Woods Hole Theater Company, Cape Cod Theatre Company and Wellfleet Actors Theatre (WHAT). Each member of the quartet chose a local playwright to write a new play, with the four works performed in staged readings and at a final festival. Other collaborations include partnerships with local cultural centers and the Cape Cod Symphony Orchestra.

By 2004, after a two-year construction project, the group had built a nine-thousand-square-foot space to house its Main Stage and gallery. The next decade saw a series of renovation projects, including renovation of a garage on the property to better house educational programming and conversion of a building into the Black Box Theater.

A note about the Black Box: The first production in the space was Henrik Ibsen's *Ghosts*, which stands as a scathing commentary on nineteenth-century morality. Since that first show, the company has used the space when it wants to create a feeling of intimacy, bringing the audience into the action of a

Above: Cotuit Center for the Arts production of *Company*, 2013. *Alan Trugman Photography*.

Left: Cotuit Center for the Arts production of *Steel Magnolias*, 2016. *Alan Trugman Photography*.

production. A good example is a recent production of *The Dixie Swim Club*, during which audience members felt they were invited into the lives of the five women in the cast. A number of other theaters in the area—including the WHAT and the Tilden Arts Center at Cape Cod Community College—have similar facilities, allowing them to stage large ensemble pieces on a main stage and up-close and personal productions in the smaller space.

The center is continuing building and renovation projects, with the eventual goal "to be Cape Cod's answer to Lincoln Center," Kuehn says, referring to Gotham's arts metropolis. In the not-too-distant future, the group hopes to construct a four-hundred-seat main stage and an outdoor space.

"There have been times when I've looked out and wondered if we would ever fill the parking lot for a production. Now we clearly need more space. Recently, we had 140 people audition for *Mary Poppins*. That's how much a part of the community and theater world we have become," Kuehn says.

Now, a short ferry ride takes us to the islands of Nantucket and Martha's Vineyard, islands drenched in theater history.

7

THEATER ON THE ISLANDS

DRENCHED IN HISTORY

So we made it to Cape Cod's bridges on our theater tour, but we're not quite done. Just a few miles out into the Atlantic stand two more outposts of the theater world: Nantucket and Martha's Vineyard. You may think that the Islands are strictly retreats meant for mindless relaxation on the beach and tours of the Vineyard's gingerbread houses.

Think again. The Islands' theater history is as rich and fertile as the fishing grounds that surround them. You'll find on these islands everything from light comedy, to experimental works and readings, to children's theater, to Shakespeare. In fact, the Islands—much like Provincetown on the Cape—have always attracted artists and celebrities, proving the perfect environment for theater to flourish.

Here's a look at the history of theater on Cape Cod's windswept islands

THEATRE WORKSHOP OF NANTUCKET: A DRAMATIC HISTORY

It's sometimes hard to pinpoint the beginning of a Cape and Islands theater company; one group often morphs into another, creating a long and varied history. That's certainly the case with the Theatre Workshop of Nantucket (TWN). The company's first season as TWN was 1956, but—like all theater culture on Nantucket—its genesis really goes back to the end of the nineteenth century.

As the artists' colony in Provincetown was making history, another colony across Nantucket Sound was taking root. Here's how a July 23, 2015 article, "Creating Magic in Sconset," on the site Yesterday's Island, Today's Nantucket (www.yesterdaysisland.com/0723201512-creating-magic-in-sconset), describes the colony.

> *The 'Sconset Actors Colony dates back to the late 1800s, when there was no air conditioning on Broadway. When the New York City theatres closed their doors for the sweltering summer months, some of the actors traveled to Hollywood. Other Broadway actors took a ferry from Manhattan to New Bedford, a train from New Bedford to Cape Cod, then a ferry from the Cape to Nantucket, and finally another train to Siasconset, where they would set up shop in this charming town. Known as the "Actors Colony" on Nantucket, these dedicated, big name Broadway actors pooled their money together and built a "hall of amusement" with tennis courts, a bowling alley, and most importantly a stage known as the "Sconset Casino."*

Fast forward to 1939, when Margaret Fawcett Barnes, whose show business parents had been part of the 'Sconset Colony, began a professional theater group, the Fawcett Players. The next year, she bought and renovated a warehouse, creating the Straight Wharf Theatre. Barnes and her husband, Robert Wilson, produced their own works, along with those of local playwright Austin Strong. Generally, the plays were based on stories from the island's history. The Players performed in the summer until 1950, with the theater going dark during the off-season. (A number of attempts to incubate new off-season groups proved unsuccessful.)

Finally, someone with the solid professional background needed to get a group up and running entered the Nantucket theater scene. Joseph "Mac" Dixon, a Broadway-trained actor and director, came to the island with his friend Jane Wallach, who just happened to be well connected to the New York arts community (and apparently knew how to tap into its coffers). Wallach secured $2,000 in funding to rent the Wharf Theatre from Barnes in the winter season, and the Theatre Workshop of Nantucket was born.

TWN's first season, from October 1956 to April 1957, featured four productions of Broadway hits of the previous decades and incorporated island talent in all aspects of the production. The first production was *Heaven Can Wait*, a 1938 Harry Segall play that was the basis for the 1941 film *Here Comes Mr. Jordan* and the 1978 film starring Warren Beatty. Reviewers of the time gave the first season high marks, boding well for the new group's future.

In 1966, the Wharf Theatre changed hands. Luckily, the new owners granted TWN use of the theater rent-free year-round for ten years, as long as the group paid the theater's maintenance fees and taxes. For the next several years, the company flourished, producing plays in the winter that would run again in repertory in the summer, with a cast of locals and off-islanders.

In 1973, TWN launched its first season with professional Equity casts, which proved a financially crippling undertaking for the small company. A rival theater, Nantucket Stage Company, then took over the summer lease for the Straight Wharf Theatre, leaving TWN without a stage for its 1975 summer season. Then, on April 19, the building burned to the ground. According to theater legend, a crew member from the local high school's senior class (which had just finished performing at the site) had marked the theater's walls with the Book of Daniel's prediction of the fall of Babylon.

For the next few years, the company went in search of a new home. According to the theater's online history, during that time, Dixon rallied the troops, saying, "A theater is not a building; it is the people who make a theater." Eventually, the group found a home in Nantucket's First Congregational Church's Bennett Hall, building a permanent theater in the hall. Artistic director Richard Cary oversaw the construction, resigning in 1984 to start Actors Theatre of Nantucket. Local artist Warren Krebs then began his tenure as artistic director, renewing TWN's educational programming and taking on more challenging productions.

Krebs directed the company until 1997, with local Nantucket playwright Kate Stout taking the reins in 2001, reaching out to the community with new mystery dinner theaters and free performances for seniors and students. Then, in 2004, as Actors Theatre closed after twenty years, TWN took on their Methodist Church lease (the performance space now known as Centre Stage) and brought Jane Karakula on as artistic director. Her tenure lasted until 2009, when John Shea—who had begun his acting career at TWN and went on to success on Broadway, in film and TV—became artistic director. According to the company's history, "Shea brought a new energy to the theater, launching initiatives such as the Staged Reading Series, in partnership with the Nantucket Atheneum."

In 2014, Shea took on the role of artistic director emeritus, with Justin Cerne coming in as artistic director. Cerne describes the company in its current incarnation as a regional theater, with local casts taking to the stage in the off-season and professionals from major markets, including of course New York, coming in to supplement local casts and crews in the summer.

In describing the annual calendar, Cerne says, "We try to appeal to a wide audience of islanders, with something for everyone." For example, the 2017 season featured *Mere Mortals* by David Ives, in which three construction workers share secrets over lunch on a skyscraper's girder; Neil Simon's *Barefoot in the Park*; *Fully Committed* by Becky Mode, which ranks as one of the top ten most-produced plays in the country; *Mamma Mia!*; Albee's *Who's Afraid of Virginia Woolf?*; and *The Sound of Music*.

The company also features a series of free staged readings and a number of workshops, geared to both students and adults. Cerne says the group will continue to offer productions and special programming that challenge both casts and audiences. "Actors and audiences should stretch their artistic muscles. We try to constantly remind them that there's a world beyond the island."

In concluding its history, the company writes (www.theatrenantucket.org):

TWN's founders believed that a community wasn't complete without quality theatre and the longevity and endurance of TWN is a testament to this. After sixty-plus years of readings, plays, classes, lectures, concerts, dances, classics, new works, musicals, community collaborations, and more, we are very grateful to be able to continue to speak to people from the stage, and we are excited to meet the future at the theatre.

Nantucket Dreamland: A Dream Come True on the Island

The name *Dreamland* brings to mind old dance halls bathed in big-band music or movie theaters where silent movies played across the screens. In the case of Nantucket Dreamland, you would be right; there was a period when the building that now houses the Nantucket Dreamland Theater was the place where people on the island went to see their favorite silent-movie stars, first saw the talkies and, eventually, enjoyed more modern, first-run movies. But today, it is a modern entertainment complex.

But, actually, the building was erected in 1832 as a Quaker meetinghouse and around the same period used for open meetings in support of the abolition of slavery. Then it became a straw-hat factory, then a roller-skating rink in 1880. In 1883, the building, then known as Atlantic Hall, actually had a moving day. It was dismantled and moved to Brant Point, where it became part of the Nantucket Hotel.

Nantucket Dreamland production. *Courtesy Dreamland staff.*

Then, in 1905, the building was purchased by new owners and, in 1906, floated back across the harbor to its present location, where it was reopened as Smith and Blanchard's Moving Picture Show. In 1911, the space was renamed the Dreamland Theatre and added vaudeville entertainment to its movie fare. Renovated and reopened in 1922, the Dreamland was a center for entertainment for more than eighty years. That made it particularly heart-wrenching for islanders when, in 2006, the building was boarded up and in desperate need of a new owner.

A group of investors who came together as the Nantucket Dreamland Foundation came to the rescue. The group bought the gorgeous structure in 2007 and undertook a massive renovation project while maintaining the building's historic integrity. By 2012, the group was ready to open what had become a world-class performing arts center, with a 314-seat theater on the first floor and a 125-seat theater/meeting room on the second floor, with a Harborview Room that looks directly out onto the harbor.

The center still features movies, with three screens gracing the complex. (In fact, movies play at the center 364 days a year.) And, in keeping with the building's history as a community meeting space, it hosts a series called

Dreamland Conversations, which has featured the likes of Vice President Joe Biden, Senator John Kerry and news personality Leslie Stahl. Then there is a series of live broadcasts from world-renowned entertainment venues— for instance, the Bolshoi Ballet and London's National Theater. And, most important for our history, it is home to the Nantucket Dreamland Theater.

Like the complex that serves as its home, the theater company emphasizes family entertainment. In fact, during the building's renovation, a tent was erected on the grounds as the site of children's productions. "There were children's productions under the tent before the building was even fully renovated. That effectively made Dreamland Theater a part of the new Dreamland [complex]," says Joe Hale, executive director of Nantucket Dreamland.

That was the seed for the group's commitment to present works "appropriate for families," says Hale. That could mean productions ranging from *To Kill a Mockingbird* to *Peter Pan*, complete with performers flying across the stage. And the group works with the local school systems to match programming to curriculum. Besides productions in spring and fall featuring professional, Equity actors, the company runs a children's camp in

Nantucket Dreamland production. *Courtesy Dreamland staff.*

Nantucket Dreamland production of *To Kill a Mockingbird. Courtesy Dreamland staff.*

the summer, where, according to Hale, young people "not only learn about theater, they also learn self-confidence." The group also brings in students for special screenings of classics, for instance *Hamlet* at London's National Theatre and *Of Mice and Men*. The events also feature a discussion period during intermission.

"We realize young people on the island don't have a lot of opportunities, so we do what we can to expose them to theater and the arts," Hale says.

In keeping with a longstanding Cape and Islands tradition of support for theater and the arts, generous islanders have made the group's programming possible, with an endowment funding some activities, Hale says. This kind of support is, after all, the Cape and Islands way.

THE WHITE HERON THEATRE COMPANY

A newer member of the Cape and Islands theater scene, the White Heron Theatre Company found its way to Nantucket, because the island "offers an incomparably stunning natural setting and a pace-of-life suited to creative reflection and the development of great new work," according to the company's site (www.whiteherontheatre.org).

The company was established in 2004 by actor-director Lynne Bolton and noted theater educator Earle Giser, associate dean of the Yale School of Drama for nearly twenty years. They were determined to create an ensemble-driven company of artists. (The term *ensemble-driven* means that, throughout a production, a cast works together to create a unified whole through integration of communication and response to one another. The theory is that, through a shared vision of the piece, the cast makes the whole work stronger, giving each cast member the security to deepen his own performance level.)

The company was established in New York, then moved to Nantucket in 2012, where it presents full productions in the summer season, offering occasional programming and an educational program in the off-season. Bolton continues as founder and artistic director, with Michael Kopko as executive director. The group's stated goal is to present "text-centric, ensemble work and collaborations—encompassing classical, contemporary and new plays that speak to audiences in timeless ways."

For its 2018 season, the group staged the Drama Desk–nominated musical *Daddy Long Legs*, Noël Coward's comedy *Private Lives* and two new plays: Calvin Trillin's *About Alice* and a world premiere of the new play *Evanston Salt Costs Climbing*. The company also touts its collaborations with world-class organizations, including the Long Wharf Theatre, the Edinburgh Fringe and the Folger Shakespeare Library in Washington, D.C.

As a final note, the group says it is dedicated to "making theater truly transformative."

MARTHA'S VINEYARD PLAYHOUSE: THEATER IN ONE OF THE ISLAND'S HISTORIC SPACES

In the town of Vineyard Haven on Martha's Vineyard, Martha's Vineyard Playhouse is a study in contrasts. It occupies a building that is almost two hundred years old, yet it offers a fare that is often new and experimental, with a little bit of Shakespeare thrown in for "measure for measure" (if you'll pardon the pun).

The building that now houses Martha's Vineyard Playhouse was built in 1833 on pastureland donated by Captain William Daggett III. (A native of Tisbury, he was part of the rich whaling history of the island. He embarked

Martha's Vineyard Playhouse's building façade. *Courtesy MVP staff.*

on a number of voyages—first as a mariner, then as captain of his own ship—beginning around 1815. Destinations included the Azores, the Cape Verde Islands, New Zealand, Samoa, Hawaii, Mexico and the northwest coast of the United States.) The building was originally constructed for $2,000 and was dedicated on July 11, 1833, as a Methodist Meetinghouse and used as such until 1845. In 1855, the building was sold for use as a public meetinghouse and named Capawock Hall. At this time, the structure was raised from one to two stories with a market on the first floor. The first Episcopal Church service on Martha's Vineyard was held there on December 24, 1862, and during that period, the hall was used for weddings and community suppers.

In 1895, the local chapter of the Masons bought the Capawock Hall after losing its own building in the great fire of 1883, which destroyed scores of buildings in the town. The building was purchased for "a considerable sum" and remodeled. According to an early document about the building, "The interior is finished throughout with southern yellow pine bead board and [it] is one of the best suburban lodges in the state."

The building was used until 1982 as a Masonic Lodge and was initially dubbed the Vineyard Association of Drama and Art when Eileen Wilson and Isabella McKamy Blake founded the theater. The name was subsequently changed to Vineyard Playhouse and is now officially the Martha's Vineyard Playhouse. (Note: Eileen is the mother of Toby Wilson, whom we introduced in the Chapter 5 section on Eventide Theatre Company. This is another example of how Cape Cod theater almost literally gets into the DNA of families, prompting one family member after another to take to the stage.)

The partners bought and converted the Masonic Lodge, designing the upstairs space as a black box theater with flexible staging options and the downstairs as a gallery/reception area. Wilson was artistic director until 1994, establishing the foundation that guides the professional theater to this day, successfully producing a professional season of five plays in the summer and assisting with introducing Shakespeare to the Tisbury Amphitheater. In a May 31, 2010 article at the time of Wilson's death, the *Vineyard Gazette* writer Julia Wells noted, "[She] saw it through a series of painful financial struggles, all the while unwavering in her vision for a professional community theatre populated by a mix of Equity actors and Vineyard amateurs."

In that same article about that first, foundational season at the theater, the *Gazette*'s Wells wrote:

> *The theatre opened for its first summer season on July 2, 1982. The shows staged that summer were an eclectic dramatic mix that would set the marquees for the playhouse of the future; in addition to the Wilde play, (The Importance of Being Earnest), in July there was a one-man show based on George Bernard Shaw's life called* My Astonishing Self, *performed as a benefit by Broadway actor Donal Donelly. August brought a production of Jules Feiffer's comedy* Knock Knock, *followed by the musical* Godspell *performed by the Connecticut Theatre Acting Company, and concluding with an original cabaret written and directed by Ms. McKamy titled* Billie and Steve. *Mrs. Wilson and her partner called in all their chips as they toiled to launch the playhouse of their dreams.*

Wilson came to the Vineyard theater project with hands-on experience in creating a working theater. She had previously lived in Westport, Connecticut, where for much of its history the Westport Community Theatre had no home of its own, using shared spaces all over the county for its productions. So Wilson helped to convince the town to convert part of a closed elementary school into a community arts center. The result was a flexible-use space that included a 150-seat black box theater that could be converted into a gallery space for visual arts. The theater space has been in continuous use since its design in 1978.

The theater's co-founder also worked with community members in developing a permanent collection of plays at the Vineyard Haven Library in honor of Lillian Hellman, who has often been called the greatest American female playwright. Hellman lived on the Vineyard until her death in 1984, and longtime island residents will tell you she may have also been the meanest American playwright. Stories abound about her shabby treatment of everyone from employees to serving people at restaurants, and there is an oft-told tale of her shuffling down the street in her later years with a cigarette hanging from her mouth.

Wilson was also a playwright in her own right, with five works to her credit, including *'Til the Boys Come Home* about her life in Scotland during World War I, and a musical based on the life of suffragette Victoria Woodhull, who—way back in the nineteenth century—presaged Hillary Clinton as the first American woman to run for president.

In 1993, the Vineyard Playhouse purchased the building, and two years later, MJ Bruder Munafo, who had served for ten years as managing and producing director under Wilson, took the mantle as artistic and executive director, a position she has held to this printing. The new director brought to the position significant directing and stage management experience, with a list of productions under her belt, including *The Grapes of Wrath*, *To Kill a Mockingbird*, *Our Town*, *Proof*, *A Midsummer Night's Dream*, *The Laramie Project*, *Master Harold and the Boys* and *The Children's Hour*. In her current role, the director has managed more than 250 plays, with productions offered on- and off-season.

To date, according to Bruder Munafo, the building has been completely gutted and literally rebuilt. Situated in the center of the Vineyard Haven Harbor Historic District, it now features seating for 100 indoors and 125 in the Tisbury amphitheater. "We're really not a traditional summer theater. We stage productions year-round, making us more of a regional theater," she says.

Martha's Vineyard Playhouse production of *Dusty and the Big Bad World*, 2017. *Courtesy MVP staff.*

A note about the company's mainstage: It is the Patricia Neal Stage, named in honor of the Oscar- and Tony Award–winning actress. Neal was a summer resident of Edgartown (another Vineyard town), where she summered until her death in 2010, and was, according to Bruder Munafo, a stalwart supporter of the Playhouse "and a good friend." When she was just twenty-one, in 1947, Neal won a Tony and a New York Drama Critic's Circle Award for her performance in Lillian Hellman's *Another Part of the Forest*. It's an interesting twist of fate that both Neal and Hellman eventually chose the Vineyard as a retreat from the rigors of Broadway and Hollywood. This is but another example of the richness celebrities have lent to the Cape Cod and Islands' theater community.

The Playhouse company maintains an incredibly ambitious calendar, averaging fifteen productions a year, with an emphasis on new works. "We're very interested in historical pieces, especially anything about the history of the island," Bruder Munafo says.

The calendar also always includes fully staged works from Shakespeare's canon presented in the outdoor amphitheater in Tisbury. And speaking of Shakespeare, the company's off-season calendar includes what Munafo calls "truncated and contemporary" versions of the Bard's work, as part of a series called Shakespeare for the Masses, which sports

Martha's Vineyard Playhouse production of *Hamlet. Courtesy MVP staff.*

the tagline "Quick & Painless & Free." The group promoted the 2015 production of the mini-version of *Julius Caesar*: "Think our senate is full of back-stabbers? Check out how they did things in Ancient Rome." (Pun apparently intended.)

The amphitheater is also the site of children's productions, part of a program that also includes summer camps for beginners and accomplished young performers. The company's mission statement describes its commitment to transforming the lives of both children and adults.

> *We believe that theater has the power to transform lives. We see it all the time, starting with the very young. Children who participate in theater learn to express themselves, learn the value working cooperatively with others, and grow in self-confidence. And adults who act in or simply enjoy plays are entertained or provoked, challenged or transported to places they can only dream of. And when, in the quiet darkness, free from outside*

distractions, we watch the fictional lives of others unfold on stage, it alters the way we think and feel about our own lives.

Peering into the future, Bruder Munafo says the group hopes to expand its campus, creating more space for visiting actors and equipment, while "creating an endowment that will secure our operation for years to come."

Back to the Mainland

Clearly, the theater history of the islands off Cape Cod's shores is as rich as their whaling past. And, as we ride the ocean waves back to the mainland, it's just as clear that each region of the Cape and Islands brings something unique and lasting to the theater community. Taken as a whole, Cape Cod theater history has been an irreplaceable part of the worldwide theater universe.

8

A FINAL NOTE

So there you have it: the dramatic tale of theater history on the tiny spit of land that was the birthplace of truly American drama. It all began with Eugene O'Neill and the Provincetown Players more than one hundred years ago, wending its way through all the towns on the Cape and Islands, creating an unbroken strand of evolution.

Despite a history rife with travails, theater continues to survive—and thrive—across the region. The theatrical descendants of the Ptown Players continue to present classical drama, contemporary hits and new, experimental works to audiences that have come to expect the highest level of performance in the Cape's historic theaters.

And, while some theater companies have found it necessary to either join forces or shape-change into cultural centers, it's clear the Cape's theater community will be thrilling and inspiring audiences for decades to come.

After all, the show must go on.

Sunset over Cape Cod Pier. *Needpix.com*.

ABOUT THE AUTHOR

 ue Mellen began her writing career as an arts, entertainment and features writer for the *Cape Cod Times*. She next went on to work in public relations, first for a regional healthcare system, then for a classic car museum. Then, after a short stint as a freelance business and technology writer, she began a content-creation firm, YourWriters, which she still operates to this day. Through her company, she has co-written and ghostwritten numerous books for a wide range of clients.

After an extended hiatus, the author has returned to her first love: reviewing the theatrical productions that grace the historic theaters of Cape Cod. Exploring the histories of the theater groups that dot the Cape has been pure joy.